Machiavellian Psychology

Theory and techniques of dark psychology, manipulation and influence

Giovanni Barone

Galatea Editions

Índex

Machiavellian Psychology

Theory and techniques of dark psychology, manipulation and influence

Giovanni Barone

Galatea Editions

WHAT IS MANIPULATION? WHAT DOES IT MEAN TO MANIPULATE?

Positioning people on inner planes rather than those which naturally correspond to them is a form of aggressive manipulation that helps generate the violence forms registered in today's current society.
Alfonso Lopez Quintás

The simplest definition of manipulation might be this one: to manipulate is to drive people at will so we can fulfill our goals. The manipulator is an artist of language and appearance, they know what is called the machiavellian psychology. Their words and their actions are apparently honest and generous, but their intentions are others and they remain hidden. The victim debates between reality and the fiction that their manipulator created for them.

When it comes to human beings, the way we relate to each other is supposed to be from equal to equal, respecting the abilities and possibility to have initiative. The philosopher, Immanuel Kant, stated that people must always be treated as ends themselves, and never as means to our selfish ends. Those who disobey this Kantian maxim, are manipulators. When you interact with a person, if instead of doing it from a position of equality, you take them as a being capable of being handled at will, you're lowering that person to the level of an object.

The situation is known by the name of sadism. Being a person who applies sadism doesn't mean being someone who acts with cruelty towards another (which is what is usually associated with being a sadist). The true meaning is lowering a person, or a group of people to the level of objects with the purpose of having domain over them. In some cases, they are lowered with cruelty, and in other cases, with a kind of tenderness that can be even more harmful.

An example of manipulation would be: when two people start to caress each other with the intention to merely gain personal pleasure and not to show each other the affection that they have for the other person (if there is affection), even though it may seem like there's a loving attitude, deep down there's a relationship of a pleasure object which can be handled at their will, meaning, a sadistic relationship. The difference lies in the intentions behind those caresses: if they include the person or exclude them.

If there is a deep feeling, the *person* will be the protagonist at all moments. But when this feeling isn't there or it's very small, they will be taken as an *object* which will generate pleasure to their counterpart, and their condition of human being is blurred in those moments. The look is considered possessive in a second place after touch, which will be in the first place when you consider the act of possession.

Another example of manipulation would be: when you enslave people with exploitative ends. There's a sadistic relationship with a cruel management which leads these slaves into thinking they don't have a way to fight back, actually believing this subduing situation is meant to be this way, in a way, they consider it right and accept it without any resistance.

A lot of ancient literature and, in some cases, not as ancient, as the one you can find corresponding to the Spaniard Gold Century, every time they referenced the seduction a man exercises on a lady, it was thought as if the gentleman had possessed her. It was related to the fact of seducing through domination, with gaining possession, with the art of tricking with beautiful words that stripped away the seduced lady's will and left her at his mercy. The seductive man didn't intend to establish a lasting relationship, what he wished was to get the lady to give herself away in mind and soul, once he achieved his goal, he abandoned her to the shame and frustration of having been mocked and discarded.

If there was a third party who wanted to stop the seductive man to achieve his goals, the problem was solved through a sword duel. Which means, the story went from the loving situation to a tragic and violent one without much controversy, like there wasn't the possibility of a more civilized resolution.

The lady became a bargaining object which could be considered lovely, fascinating, adorable, etc., but who continued to be an object with no personal thoughts or opinions.

It's quite usual to think of a person, before attacking them, as an enemy or a dangerous obstacle. This thought, whether it's conscious or not, leads to feeling free to use all the annihilation possibilities. It's a common social practice, especially in working environments.

Another way to define manipulation is to consider it a way to socially influence with the sole intention to modify the behavior and perception of others, using indirect deceiving strategies. These tricks will benefit those who use them, moving forward at other people's expenses.

In some cases, manipulation is used with the intention of benefitting the other example. The clearest example of this is the case of parents with their children so that they eat healthy food or make the right choices.

The influence that can be exercised socially is, generally, harmless and takes a place of relevance in social interaction. There's no coercive demand, no bad intention. If a person tries to exercise their influence on someone else and they resist, the former won't try to force them and there won't be any kind of consequence for the denial.

However, if the psychological manipulation is negative, their influence contains harmful techniques to push the other person once it's obvious that there's a resistance to the natural form of manipulation. When you exercise these types of mechanisms, the person who practices them is aggressive in nature, though they may seem harmless on the surface. The truth is they have the ability to be subtle, and they've also taken the time to research and know the vulnerabilities of the person they wish to manipulate.

This is an important element to take into account, the manipulative person doesn't allow their intentions to show through from the beginning, but they start the relationship in a casual way, trying to be likeable while they do their research and get to know the strong and weak points of the person who, probably, shows them empathy so that they feel confidence. When the victim finds themselves with a low guard, the manipulator will start to exercise their influence on them, wrapping them up and convincing them in order to achieve their machiavellian ends.

An example of a harmless or even positive influence would be: the publicity that encourages people to eat healthy food, regularly work out to avoid a sedentary lifestyle or to create awareness about the need to be more ecofriendly and take care of the planet.

An example of an influence that can be either harmless or destructive depending on the case would be: fashion and the clothing trends, as well as the ideas regarding body beauty considering them to be a paradigm to follow, the personal or corporate image and the need to develop muscle mass to have the much-desired athletic body. Some people follow these trends without paying much attention to them, but in other cases, there are those who suffer and even get sick for not being able to fulfill these beauty standards. There are also those who spend their entire salary on clothing and accessories to dress differently every day and be fashionable all the time.

Every time you meet a new person it's important to see how they behave with other people. If it's a person who achieves leadership or influence on others, it's necessary to be on the lookout of how their relationship with us develops. If this person manipulates others, it is to be expected that at some point they try to exercise their influence on us. Believing that they won't try to manipulate us in the entryway to manipulation.

The harmless this person seems to everyone else's eyes, the more dangerous their influence becomes. Staying sharp to avoid being manipulated will be the best way to protect not only yourself but also your loved ones who can be victims of these situations.

MANIPULATION AND PERSONALITY

HOW IS A MANIPULATIVE PERSON?

When you manage to be aware of how simple manipulating can be, you appreciate the actual reach that emotional manipulation can have. The strategies of manipulation are derivative of the already existing method of control. Generally, the person isn't aware of what is happening to them.

The most dangerous and skillful manipulators are those who plan coldly and without considering the implications it may have on the other person. They lack empathy and their only interest is to chase their own benefit. They tend to be aggressive people, opportunists, insensitive, who only think about themselves. They're wolves in sheep's clothing moving in the world harmlessly, but that, at some point, shows who they truly are.

Sometimes, these people have serious psychological disorders. When people who have a normal psyche exercise manipulation, they don't have an excuse to keep up with that attitude. Those with psychological disorders can explain their actions with their mental issues.

There are two basic types of manipulation that can be differentiated: those people who scarcely manipulate and those who constantly manipulate with a behavior that could be considered pathological. The pathological manipulator knows no other way to interact with the rest of the world.

While those who scarcely manipulate have other ways to interact aside from those who are associated with a manipulative attitude.

The emotional manipulation slowly wears out the other person, taking away their self-confidence and changing their own perceptions. This work can take time, but the degradation is inexorable, and can even be permanent, if the person doesn't react in time. The victim trusts their manipulator and this is the key of the control they exercise, since the person can even put all of their life choices in their manipulator's hands.

It's necessary to establish a difference when it comes to manipulation. The manipulator seeks to defeat, they're not interested in convincing. By convincing a person through the exposed reasons you're not manipulating. The other person considers that the exposed reasons are so valid that they make them change their mind. This attitude favors that person's growth, definitely, it elevates them because it perfected the knowledge in this subject.

But when the person accepts what the manipulator says without understanding the reasons, they adopt or bend to a gregarious behavior, determined by the person who leads them. The aggressor is shaping the minds and wills to their liking so they can achieve their goals.

A clear example of this kind of manipulation is the one exercised by religious leaders who lead their followers into reneging medicine and refusing to get a transfusion, even when their lives, or their loved ones depend on it. What their leader taught them must be fulfilled at all costs, thinking that the others are out to harm them, in this case a doctor, who is actually hoping to save their lives, but that is interpreted by the manipulated person, as an act of prejudice against their lives.

Another similar case, but which can't be considered manipulation, could be that of a salesman who orientates the customer's buy. When they guide them hoping they can get what they need, they act to the customer's favor and convenience, and not their own benefit. In that case, the customer trusts the recommendations made by the salesman for being selfless and legitimate.

When the salesman speaks in favor of a product with the sole intention of selling it, without giving much thought to the customer's necessities, they are exercising manipulation in order to achieve the sale that's going to benefit them. In this case, they set in motion a series of strategies to convince the person they are doing the best buy of their lives and that under no circumstances they should miss out on it. Actually, they limit their offer to a limited amount of time or to an established product quantity, to generate the feeling of scarcity on the customer and push them into believing they must buy the product immediately.

Another resource which is often applied is the use of an image, which triggers on the person who looks at it, pleasant feelings which they'll only be able to enjoy if they buy that product. The clearest example in this case are the cars' advertisements, where they show the vehicle being driven by a man with a beautiful lady by his side driving around dream places with background music which invites you to travel and a calm, reassuring voice which says: "Enjoy the deepest emotions".

There is no reference being made to the car at any moment, but it gives the feeling that only by driving this car you'll get everything you need and you'll achieve the status that you deserve. They seduce with the image of power, they stimulate desire, overrule the will. They don't mention how much it costs so that the rational aspects don't intervene. They just nourish the senses, the desires, the passions, and everything that has to do with the irrational aspects of the human being.

Besides, they use the social stereotype of the powerful man who is capable of catching the eye of the most beautiful woman. That is why, it's the man driving and not the woman. Once again, here the woman is an object used to get the admiration or envy of other men, proving that he is successful.

You can keep counting different adverts which have as a goal to get instinctive emotions to flourish in the spectators. If every time you go shopping you notice your attention drifts towards the products in these adverts, you must realize that you're being manipulated and the decisions you take, probably respond to the adverts you watched, without paying too much mind to them, but that were left ingrained in your subconscious. This kind of manipulation is found present in every order of life.

When you try to drag someone towards the ideas that some other person states we are facing ideological manipulation. Those who exercise this type of manipulation are known as demagogues and their influence can be highly harmful and damaging.

> Ideology, in a restrictive sense, is understood today as a set of ideas — politic, economic, religious...— that certain groups have, not so much for the rigorous conviction that those ideas truly reflect reality, but for sentimental reasons and different interests. History teaches us that, if a way of thinking is adopted and kept as an unalterable program by a political party, it gets loaded with a strong dose of emotion, but it loses on a day-to-day basis it's persuasive power. It doesn't seem to have any other choice than to impose actively as a dictatorship, or to infiltrate the public opinion in a painful way, through the use of manipulation.[1]

Unlike the manipulator, those who spread their ideas in an honest and open way are a guide or a master. Their ideas can be wrong, but they aren't deceiving at any moment. They move forward with what they consider to be truth.

Some parents believe that guiding their children with the same values that they cultivated can be considered manipulation. But it's not the case, values are being incorporated slowly, without being forced. It's about values and ideas, not ideology.

The ideological manipulation is often used for the increase in consumption and with the intention that people feel the need to overflow with possessions and the emotions they generate. This combination of manipulation in which shopping for ideological reasons is encouraged can be devastating.

Chain production is a great example of a job that pro-

---

[1] *The manipulation of man through language* - Alfonso López Quintás

duces alienation since it kills off creativity, it's repetitive and monotonous, it's recurrent and boring. It's a way to turn a person into an automaton.

Automation is the path towards good cost-effectiveness, but it turns the operating person into a piece of gear with no possibility to develop their potential. It's necessary that those repetitive processes are done by machinery, and not by people.

In other orders of life as well, you can find similar processes that act against the way the human being thinks, feels and wants. By knowing these mechanisms and how they work you'll be able to avoid falling into them and be puppets in someone else's hands so that they can use persuasion to their benefit.

The person who has the intention to manipulate, dedicates part of their time to study machiavellian psychology of the masses to understand and know how it works and how it can be used to their advantage.

Generally, the manipulator is an attractive person, charismatic, someone that's likeable because their first actions seem selfless, but this isn't anything else other than an entry point so that they're welcomed into the group they are trying to control.

People often allow themselves to be belittled just so they can achieve a feeling of belonging to what would be a status level that would definitely flatter their ego and generate a feeling of power.

A good example of this is: the influence that politicians exercise over a certain group of people in society, which they flatter on some of their elemental preferences and make campaign promises in favor of solving their unsatisfied necessities. This attitude will make this group of people feel included, taken into account and respected.

They definitely exercise fascination and this does nothing but dominate the will of those who believe in what is being promised. This group, in part, feels liberated when voting for this political leader and, later on, will feel disappointed and used when they don't fulfill their campaign promises.

On the other hand, the manipulator doesn't aim at the bottom line, or the heart of the matter, but they focus on secondary details with the intention of impressing their listeners, not to solve the problem. Their behavior tends to a single perspective of the subject, never to the full picture or an objective global view. It's common that they impoverish the language, empty it from its content or substance so they can detour attention. Besides, they use socially accepted cliches as a safe entryway.

Another important aspect that is signature of the manipulator is that they're not interested in seeking the truth, but in imposing and defeating their opponent. The language, which is ambiguous, allows the manipulator to deceive without falling into lies. For instance: if a real estate agent tries to sell a house that has small dimensions, they don't say it's small, they say it's cozy and familiar. They're not lying but they're not telling the truth either.

Frequently, the manipulative person doesn't start dialogue as a way to clear up ideas. They're not keen on debate or on spaces created to expose the different points of view, to come from opinions and to make an effort to find the truth. On the contrary, their opinion is totally partial, besides, they have a well put together speech that, in case of confrontation, they repeat as a prayer.

A manipulative person relies on the manipulated person's tendency to enhance their control. Some of these tendencies are:

- The belief that freedom is not having to face any obstacles.
- The ordinary person seeks easy and quick solutions, in the form of a recipe, if possible.
- The ordinary person has the need to avoid conflict and maintain peace. This attitude makes them feel safe.

WHICH ARE THE COMMON TRAITS OF THE MANIPULATED PERSON?

Each person has their own traits and characteristics which make them unique. Sometimes, these aspects make them prone to being manipulated. Manipulators know deeply which traits to look for in a person so that they're actions are a hundred percent effective.

Psychological characteristics of people who are prone to being manipulated:

- Insecurity and emotional frailty.
- Sensitivity.
- Empathy.
- Fear of loneliness.
- Fear of letting people down.
- Personality dependent disorders and emotional dependence.

Insecurity and emotional frailty

These are the favorite victims and, unfortunately, they're very easy to identify which also makes them easy to find, even for strangers. The behavior that identifies this type of person is that they have the tendency to be defensive in the face of the slightest attack or when they find themselves under pressure. This leads them to be easily detected in social gatherings.

The manipulator doesn't need to deeply interact with them to measure their level of insecurity. They'll do an attempt by provoking their possible target in an innocent and subtle way, analyzing their reaction. If they react in a defensive way, these people will be classified as insecure or emotionally fragile and the manipulator will start targeting them.

Other people will show social anxiety, which leads to thinking that, deep down, they're emotionally fragile too. In Social settings, they're easily detected because of their body language. These behaviors don't go unnoticed for money pit later. At this point, we must differentiate insecure people from the emotional point of view, from those which are fragile in this regard. The insecure people manifest immediately, whilst the fragile ones are apparently normal, but they break down easily when they're faced with the slightest provocation. Once the manipulator finds emotional frailty, they will use all of their tricks.

The condition of emotional frailty is, generally, temporary. Which is why, you can be the victim of an occasional manipulator who seizes the opportunity to their favor, knowing that it won't last and that his blow will be quick and certain. A person with a balanced emotional level can experience moments of frailty when dealing with a difficult situation like a breakup, grieving, a stressful moment, etc., but, despite it, this frailty is not a part of their personality.

Sensitive people

This type of personality makes the person process life and the information they receive on a deeper level, and they have the ability to distinguish the subtleties that manifest in social relationships. They possess many virtues which they're known for, they analyze their own actions and avoid hurting other people. These are people who don't feel drawn to any kind of violence, they're affected by the news of natural disasters and even avoid watching bloody scenes in movies. They can emotionally wear out when having to assimilate what someone else is feeling. They can detect someone else's mood because they are skillful when it comes to reading body language, face expressions and the variations in the voice tone.

This sensitivity is used by manipulators by faking

some emotions which try to throw this type of personality off balance. They also use their predisposition to feeling scared when dealing with stressful or threatening situations, in a way that the manipulator will pretend to provide safety and protection from these threats.

Sensitive people are introverted, they like to go unnoticed since social relationships can turn out to be stressful and exhausting to them. They are, generally, politically correct, they don't use vulgar language, they try to avoid hurting or offending others. They move with education, saying please and thanking quite frequently. Manipulators will approach them because they know that, out of education, they won't reject them and they'll try to be complacent to try and not to hurt them, making their entryway easy for them.

Empathetic people

This type of personality is very similar to the sensitive one, but with the difference that they are more in tune with other people's feelings and the social world which surrounds them. They can internalize other people's feelings to the point of making it their own. They're good as partners and also as friends because of the great empirical understanding they have about others.

Manipulators are capable of faking certain emotions to approach them, opening a communication channel. It's very easy to deceive them and, especially, to financially scam them. These are people who have a great heart and who are selfless, they're always willing to help those who need them.

They can even feel guilty because other people are suffering, even if they have nothing to do with the causes of their pain.

Fear of loneliness

It's quite frequent that people feel afraid of being alone, to the point that it can become paralyzing for some of them. This fear can lead them to keep relationships that aren't convenient for them or accept any kind of company to avoid loneliness, even a relationship of submission or abuse. They are easy prey for manipulators who approach them looking for a friendship or the ideal couple relationship, that a person who struggles with fear of loneliness won't be able to reject. When they have their full confidence, they begin with their scams. What uncovers these types of people is the level of despair they show at the beginning of a relationship. This desperation causes those who are emotionally balanced to systematically reject them.

This fear of loneliness, generally, affects women more than men for cultural reasons, since it's already known that women are taught from a very young age that they have to get married and have children and, in some cases, be obedient women so that they don't get abandoned.

People who were abandoned in childhood are prone to suffering from fear of abandonment. Besides, even if they're not afraid of loneliness, some people are afraid of being away from their loved ones and they rather keep any type of relationship with them.

Fear of letting other people down

This is a feeling that all human beings experience in a greater or lesser measure. In some cases, this fear becomes pathological. It's a fear that can be matched to the one you feel for being embarrassed or the fear of rejection, since the person places a special attention on other people's perception of them.

In some situations, this fear works for the person's, or family group's advantage, for instance, the man who becomes a hard worker so they don't disappoint their family, or the children who study a lot so they don't disappoint their parents. When this fear is directed at the wrong people, it can work against the person who has this feeling, sometimes compromising their own integrity.

Manipulators, when uncovering this weakness, will find a way to make the person feel this fear for them. For instance, they can do some favors causing the person that feeling of obligation that they'll have to fulfill whenever the manipulator asks them to.

Personality dependent disorders and emotional dependence

The dependence disorder is characterized by the fact that the person feels an extreme necessity to be looked after. This necessity makes them fearful of separating their loved ones, and they're even capable of turning into submissive and obedient people just so they can avoid the separation.

Their way of behaving suggests a need to be looked after at every moment. They behave like they're unable to do certain things and they need others to do those things for them. This behavior is called "learned impotence". This type of person often faces difficulties when making decisions, even if they're simple decisions like what to wear on a daily basis. They need the support and advice of other people constantly. They expect others to make their decisions for them and, frequently, go back and live with their parents as adults or treat their partners as if they were their mother or father.

Manipulators approach these kinds of people to generate a feeling of safety and seek to gain control over their lives. These people give in to control and it is there when the manipulator starts exercising their will on them.

This dependency can happen due to a low self-esteem or as a result of abandonment during childhood. Generally, it doesn't reach a point where medical treatment is needed, but it's a disorder that doesn't allow people to live their lives to the fullest. Generally, they tend to be nice people to deal with, since they're constantly looking for approval.

PERSUASION

Being aware of oneself and being in control of every aspect of how you think and how you react, provides you with the necessary abilities to use persuasive techniques to your benefit. You must be aware that everyone can be mentally manipulated and no one is safe from these persuasive tactics.

S.L Moore

PERSUASION PSYCHOLOGY

Currently, you can appreciate how machiavellian psychology is installed in every aspect of a human being's life. You find it on advertisements, on everyday communication, at different workplaces, at political rallies as well as religious ones, and sometimes, in our relationships with our loved ones.

A way to define persuasion is as the ability that a person has to convince the recipient to change their points of view, their beliefs or their behavior, through verbal communication.

Persuasion strategies are oriented to emotions as entryways to the thoughts. Persuasion isn't a form of mind control, it's a way of manipulating someone else's mind. It's a technique that has been studied since ancient times, being the Greek philosophers the first ones to talk about it. They studied in which way speakers used the language to focus in different ways to convey their message.

Aristotle was one of the philosophers who studied persuasion and divided it into three parts: *ethos, logos* and *pathos*. He gave the name *ethos* to the credibility that the speaker had. Aristotle noticed that when the speakers addressed the spectators with confidence and presented themselves as experts on the matter, their message was better received than those who displayed any kind of weakness, such as nervousness, stuttering or insecurity.

The second part, *logo*, which means logic, was taken into account by Aristotle because he figured out that the speech had to contain some logical aspects in which to base itself in. This reasoning makes the spectator assume that they reached a conclusion by their own deduction ability, when actually, they were skillfully led to it.

The last point, *pathos*, was defined as the emotional strategy that leads to the expected result in spectators. He understood that the speech was more effective when the audience was in the right emotional state, and in this way, they'd be easily influenced and susceptible. These aspects described by Aristotle are the main fundamentals of the persuasion used nowadays.

The person who applies this method, tries to shape to their convenience. They act with subtlety slowly changing thoughts and ideas. The best examples of this are the adverts with their jingles, slogans, the colors they used (which have been carefully studied) and the celebrities which get hired to do them. In an unconscious way, these adverts shape the consumers' minds.

You only have to imagine a person watching TV, a series or their favorite team's game, when suddenly, the adverts come. One of them talks of an exquisite burger, it's very likely that the person doesn't pay much attention to it, but in their subconscious, a necessity begins to take shape. Until that moment they didn't feel the desire to eat a burger, that desire started after the advert. That's what persuasion applied to consumption is based on.

Current researchers, based on the former studies, have focused on how persuasion works on a deep psychological level. They focus on what's the mind's reaction towards persuasion and how it's used in everyday interactions. In one of these researches, it was discovered that the use of these methods is far more common than expected.

In a normal conversation, the one who exposes their topic uses certain words, in a conscious or unconscious way, to generate an emotional response in the other person. Sometimes, it is done with the intention that the other person feels what the speaker felt when the events of the story took place. In this case, persuasion is used hoping to cause empathy in the listener. This study proves that all people are capable of using persuasion as a means to an end, even if they're not fully aware of it.

ROBERT CIALDINI'S PERSUASION PRINCIPLES

To be able to fully understand persuasive techniques and how they are used in current society, we must look into the studies of Dr. Robert Cialdini, described in his book *Influence: The Psychology of Persuasion*, published in 1984. In this book, he exposes the aspects of psychological persuasion which can be applied to marketing. It's worth mentioning that Dr. Cialdini is an Emeritus Professor of Psychology and Regents Marketing at Arizona State University.

This published work continues to be consulted by entrepreneurs, politicians and academics who saw the possibility to move towards success when following his concepts. Among the famous people who have followed his principles we can find Donald Trump, who based his political campaign on persuasion, managing to get the necessary votes to become president.

Dr. Cialdini's ability which guaranteed the success of his book was analyzing every complex aspect of psychological persuasion, and reducing them into simple concepts that he divided in 6 points:

1. Reciprocity: it's the action taken by the persuader when they offer something in return that, perhaps, the other person didn't need until it was offered to them.
2. Compromise and consistency: in this point, the persuader tries to obtain the fidelity or loyalty of the persuaded person. It's analyzed how to make sure that the person who made a decision stays in that same state.
3. Social proof, also called "social informative influence": it refers to leading to mass or gregari-

ous behavior, which is the tendency to follow the crowd.

4. Taste or likeability: in this point, it is analyzed how a person can be persuaded by the simple fact that they like the person who's persuading them.

5. Authority: in this point the analysis is focused on how a person can persuade simply for being a person in a position of power.

6. Scarcity: this point is based on the fact that knowing that a product is scarce will make people want it.

RECIPROCITY PRINCIPLE

The reciprocity principle is born from the human being's social nature. When a person receives a favor, it's very likely that they feel the need to return that favor or pay it off in some way. A notable example of the use of this principle is carried out by the Hare Krishna, who makes a gift, for instance a flower or a book and, when accepting this gift, they request a donation in return. Acting this way has increased the donations they receive in a very significant way.

Mostly, when people do a favor, they don't accept a payment in return, but they conform with the gratefulness the other person feels for them. This selfless attitude can be taken as a diminishment of the importance of the favor and the person who received said favor feels like they don't owe anything. A way to not diminish the importance of the favor is saying: "It doesn't matter, I know you'd do the same for me". This type of answer causes a feeling of debt on the other person.

Then, reciprocity was defined by Dr. Cialdini as the action of offering some benefit to the person that you're trying to persuade. You offer something that they might need or not, but the moment you offer it to them, the persuaded person feels like they need it, even if they don't know it. In this way, the victim feels in debt because the persuader, using their manipulation technique, caused this feeling. The victim thinks the other person acts selflessly even though, actually, it's not the case. The person feels grateful to their persuader because they offered them something they wanted. It's likely that they believe they are working to achieve a final prize and this leads them to enhance their connection with their persuader.

This reciprocity technique has been studied and used in marketing for the great results it can get. You start the adverts with the image of a scenery or a famous person and then you connect it to the product. In this way, very subtly, thinking about the product references the celebrity and the person wants to acquire the product due to that connection they feel to them. Even though most people are aware of the manipulation that adverts do, they are still very effective and they are capable of achieving the results expected from them. It's like, unconsciously, it gives them a sense of security to walk into these kinds of games.

Pavlov proved that dogs, when being fed after listening to a little bell, associated this sound to food. Once this connection was established, the animals started their salivation process when listening to the bell. These reflexes he called the "Pavlov's conditioned reflexes".

The human being is also susceptible to this kind of association. A renowned advertisement overlaps a beer's logo on different pleasant activities: sailing, skiing, or snuggling with a partner. In this way, positive feelings towards this beer were improved, with a corresponding increase in consumption.

Another example of the use of conditioned reflexes is the experiment that was performed on thirty people in the following way: they presented eight different happy faces repeatedly to this group of people that was thirsty before making them taste a new kind of soda. This led them to consume the soda in greater quantities, paying even three times its original price for it. The people who participated in this experiment weren't aware of these mechanisms at any moment.

These connections can be used in a positive way as well. For instance, when a person sets themselves a goal which is difficult to achieve, like losing weight or performing a physical activity. To avoid the frustration of not achieving said goal, whether it is for forgetfulness or because the intentions were divided due to situations that continued to come up, there's a series of affirmation which can be used. These affirmations are designed to help people achieve their goals, seeking to accomplish a better predisposition when it comes to their surroundings, so that it's more favorable to achieve the goal and perform coherent actions that lead to the fulfillment of the task.

For example: "when it's 8 in the morning I will be in an exercising position so I can tone my muscles". The effectiveness level of these affirmations that we set for ourselves is really high and it leads to believing they can actually work.

SOCIAL PROOF PRINCIPLE

The social proof principle is one of the most powerful ones and it is based on the social consensus. The best way to understand it is to imagine that in a certain place, there are two bars that you can go to. The first one is filled with people, there's even people waiting outside and the parking lot is full. The second one is empty. Despite this situation, nine out of ten people will go to the one that is full. The reason why they pick it is precisely because everyone is there. Generally, human beings think that if the place is full, it means it has the better quality, instead of thinking that they have a great marketing team which generated this necessity.

This type of behavior is called social proof. There's a great number of marketing companies who use promoting phrases like: "We're 200.000 and growing, join this great family". These phrases, along with the testimony or opinions of those people who use the product, guarantee a great marketing campaign, since those who aren't quite sure of buying the product, receive the extra push necessary to make up their minds.

This type of behavior was proven through conducted studies where they concluded that a product positions itself in a great spot for the simple fact that it has social consensus.

Besides, it was also noticed how there was a certain preference for those products that were advertised in a subtle way, instead of those which were advertised in an exaggerated manner.

People have the knowledge that marketing influences their own judgment, but still, they allow themselves to be manipulated by advertisements.

When the exposure to a product's advertisement becomes exaggerated and abuses the attempts to achieve social consensus, it produces the opposite effect on the consumer. This excess acts as a reminder of the effect that marketing has.

Another way of correcting the marketing influence is to do some previous reasoning which comes from an established necessity. This way can be slower and more difficult to fulfill, since it leaves the pleasant feelings associated with the advertised products aside. It requires a strength of will. For instance, going shopping to the supermarket with the idea of getting those products which are healthy and that have a determined number of calories. Then, while the person shops, they check the labels to know what they're buying and they leave aside the advertised products because they don't fulfill the goals they set.

And will also be considered, then being carried away by advertisements and what is socially accepted, prevents us from falling into exhaustive analysis. These analyses don't only take too much time, but also energy and motivation. This is why most times we don't perform them. If a person doesn't have the time, analysis ability and the will to make an effort to weigh out the options, it's unlikely that they'll sit down to make an analysis of every single product they wish to acquire.

That is why we take the quicker road which isn't always negative. In certain opportunities it can be efficient. In other occasions, it leads to detouring the person from their goals. By having to make a decision it can happen that in that moment you don't have your full thinking ability, whether it's because you're tired or stressed out, in these cases, it's not the time to make decisions because they wouldn't receive the necessary balanced evaluation.

Certain advertisements are broadcasted in schedules where you could even assume that they aren't commercials. However, in those moments people go to their television to rest from their day and their energy is low enough to allow into their minds all of the emotional tricks that advertisements use: attractive announcements, limited offers, charismatic presenters, etc.

Advertising isn't the only area that uses this effect. Much was experienced in this regard. Researchers investigating the effects of restful sleep on people found that if a soldier is well-rested, they can defy the orders to fire on hospitals and civilian targets. If these same soldiers go twenty-for to thirty-six hours without sleep, they will not only obey orders without question, but they will be willing to fire on any target that comes their way. The same thing happens with police questioning. An innocent person can plead guilty just because they weren't able to resist the pressure of hours of interrogation that wear out their minds.

AUTHORITY PRINCIPLE

This principle highlights the fact that people, in a way, enjoy obeying the authorities. In some cases, you might argue that they like it to the point that they don't even question what they ask of them, even if what they're being requested is clearly doubtful or unethical.

An example of this happened when a journalist placed a poster on an ATM which said: "ATM out of service. Deliver the deposits to the policeman". This supposed policeman, all dressed up, was standing next to the ATM with an authoritarian appearance. In just two hours he got from the people who went to the ATM over two thousand pesos in cash and checks, aside from social security numbers, credit cards, account numbers, codes, PIN and many personal data that shouldn't be divulged. There was only one person that doubted and refused to deliver their deposits to the policeman. When they uncovered their deception to these victims, they asked them why they delivered their information and money so easily, they replied that they did it because there was a policeman there. This proved that authority isn't related to force but rather to appearances.

In a different research, the possibility to do a course which will allow you to transform yourself into a very successful entrepreneur was divulged. Two options were offered: in the first one, the person who taught the course had a refined and athletic appearance, drove a car that many people desire and was dressed neatly with an expensive suit. In the second option, the person in charge of teaching the course was obese, scruffy looking, dressed in an ordinary suit and driving a car in poor conditions. It was observed that nine out of ten people chose the first option because the stereotype of a successful entrepreneur aligned with the image of the first option's speaker.

It's also proven that if you go in a place where you're generally stopped by a guard with a body language that demonstrates determination and authority at the entrance, this guard won't stop you even if they've never seen you go in before. The mere fact of seeing the confidence with which you walk in will make them doubt and think you have a position of power.

This is the same way in which advertisement works. In general, people aren't able to give a conscious response to a political speech since it all indicates that attention is being directed at the least relevant stuff like their personal attractiveness, charisma, the image they portray, etc.

Other conditions that are found in everyday life and that prevent a correct approach to the decision-making process, have to do with the multiple factors which act as distractions and that cloud the reasoning ability such as the amount of information that can be accessed thanks to the Internet. It's something that overwhelms and, sometimes, overrules the ability to decide. To this we must add the number of mobile devices that have become essential for our lives, or so we've been led to believe, each with their respective message notifications that can't be left unanswered so that we're not disconnected from the virtual world.

Communicators know that automatic and socially approved associations work and that there are very few possibilities that the audience will refute their products on conscious debates. Other examples of these tactics are:

- If you want people to buy an Irish wine, you put as background music a melody that is characteristic of this country.
- If you want people to buy an expensive item, you can make the prices higher and claim it is an exclusive product.
- If you want people to try out a new product, you can ask them if they like adventure.
- If you want people to feel comfortable, you can offer them a warm beverage.
- If you want people to work for their goals, you can show a picture of a runner who's holding a medal.

In this type of tricks, you must take into account that what you're aiming for must be aligned to the motivation given. If what you seek doesn't align with the motivation, this will be fruitless. Meaning, this incentive will make the person predisposed to perform what was previously established.

LIKEABILITY PRINCIPLE

People recognize that advertisement can influence their judgment, but they don't do anything to correct this until they are reminded of the potential source of conditioning.

Robert Cialdini

This principle proves that people are likely to be influenced by those people who they like. A way to prove this are salesmen that go door to door. Those who get more sales are not only those who visit the most clients, but also those who are able to establish a relationship of trust with them by investing the most amount of time. Those who were able to achieve the potential customer's liking also managed to influence them into buying their products.

This principle is based on the research conducted by the psychologist Daniel Kahneman, who won the Nobel Memorial Prize in Economic Sciences presenting his work along with Vernon Smith in which they laid the foundations for the beginning of a new discipline: "Neuro-economics". In it, it was shown that people not only prefer to buy from those who they like, but they are also capable of paying higher prices. In some cases, these principles seem to not follow any logical paths, which speaks of the human being's irrationality and that it's in this way that they make their decisions most times.

Perhaps, you wish to change that way of making decisions and get rid of the influence these principles have on us. The sole fact of remembering that we're under their influence is good to help us be aware and escape from it. In decision making, the mood and the weather also have an influence. In a research conducted via telephone, people expressed they felt a lot better when they were consulted on sunny days than when they were consulted on cloudy days. The rate varied by twenty percent.

In this same study, it was proven that after answering the question, they were consulted on which weather they had at the moment, and realizing the influence that it had, they modified their answers to one that was closer to reality. Their answers became more objective and accurate.

On one occasion, Hollywood director Gregory Ratoff said: "Let me ask you a question, for your information". This affirmation may seem absurd or it might be considered as nonsense said by mistake, it can have a background which isn't analyzed at plain sight: it's a question that can have interest information for the recipient, it can lead them to remember a knowledge they already possessed on their minds and that didn't hold any relevance until the speaker mentioned it.

That which may seem harmless proves that you can direct someone's attention to unexpected places, allowing for perception to, innocently, redirect their attention to where it's needed.

Hollywood studios have put this principle into practice since its inception. They position products in the films they make, aside from charging the brands for the use of their products by their characters. The prices they handle for this sort of advertisement are quite high, especially considering if the person who uses the product is extremely famous.

This type of product use is known as: *product placement.*

It has also been shown that the more noticeable the connections are, the more effective they become. A study conducted with the television series *Seinfeld,* showed that when the character named the product out loud, the highest rates of recalling by the audience were produced compared to other moments where the product was placed in the background. However, the researchers who conducted this study also asked the audience to check in a list those products they would eventually buy and, to their surprise, the least checked were those which were ostentatiously advertised. A forty-seven percent of the audience chose those who were advertised in a subtle way and those who were noticeably advertised, were chosen by twenty-seven percent. It is clear that if the advertising's influence is remembered, it is due to an exaggerated exposure of the product.

AFFILIATION NEED

In general, the human being is a social animal. They tend to live in society and need to feel accepted and wanted in the group in which they develop. The emotional development that the individual has, as well as their affective story and the affections with which they surrounded themselves play a fundamental role here.

The affiliation need is defined as the actions that are born from the search that tries to cover the needs that have to do with the individual's general wellbeing and their relationship with other people. In this search, personal development and the need for self-realization are also included. Rejection by others, isn't accepted by most people. This is why they do all that's in their power to please others, putting together a pleasant behavior, showing that they share common interests and much more.

In many cases, society's general approval is sought by trying to align the concepts that one has with those who hold together the society in which we live in. The likeability and reciprocity techniques are a complement to this affiliation need that the human being has. People who use persuasion know of this association and they take advantage of all the influence they have on others so that they can achieve their goals.

The people who try to influence others know this need to be certain of their choices. Therefore, they will offer their solutions trying to prevent the person from thinking too much. On the other hand, the person who receives the solutions, will feel that the person who is influencing them is right in their views and will put them at stake fearing to lose a deal if they don't.

It's important to understand that the human being wants to build, show, and protect the vision they have of themselves and the place they occupy in the world and the society in which they operate. They need to build their self-esteem, their beliefs, make them known, align them with other people's and maintain them through time as long as they consider them valid.

All people, without exceptions, seek to have precision in their concepts and achieve consensus between their ideas and other people's ideas, thus obtaining affiliation with them. The language they will use to accomplish the alignment of concepts will adapt to the recipient or recipients' characteristics. In the same way, the message will also be structured considering who it's directed to. Building a message in a persuasive way requires very well studied rules.

FORMS OF PSYCHOLOGICAL MANIPULATION, FROM THE MOST NOBLE TO THE MOST MACHIAVELLIAN

THE IMPORTANCE OF THE GAZE

Avoiding the influence of the human gaze is something that few people can accomplish. Some of them have a way of looking that naturally attracts, specially, those who are able to hold a gaze without blinking for a reasonable period of time. That gaze has to be the protection of the thought they try to convey. Some animals, as well, know how to exercise this fascination on their prey, paralyzing them with the sole impact of an intense gaze.

To convince someone about something it's important to look them in the eye, but in a way that the other person doesn't read as a challenge. A challenging look can turn out to be annoying, to the point that the other person feels the need to look away. In this case, the necessary contact to reach the fascination levels the speech requires wouldn't be accomplished.

The most subtle way of beginning the fascination through the gaze would be to use it to achieve an influence when speaking about topics that aren't very transcendental. In this stage, you should not display any rush or impatience and you must listen to what another has to say. Just like it's necessary to avoid the rush, it's also necessary to avoid shyness, the false modesty to achieve a direct gaze that denotes frankness and that is directed at the base of the nose rather than straight to the eyes. It will give the feeling that it's being directed at the eyes and it will be less intense, therefore, it won't cause as much discomfort in the receiver.

These steps are necessary when you're looking to influence others with your gaze. By doing it directly the most likely thing to happen is that the interlocutor will become defensive and the efforts made will be useless.

The story goes, a young man wanted to solicit the help from a mediator so that he interceded between him and his friend with the intention of accomplishing a business to his favor and to his friend's detriment. This young man believed he could convince the mediator through his gaze, but he found that he was a strong-willed man who was aware of such tricks. So, the mediator decided to teach this young man a lesson using his own techniques, but with more discretion. The young man wasn't prepared to receive a counterattack so he ended up defeated and embarrassed to admit his attempted manipulation.

The influence that a gaze can have is powerful and it's a great ally when making a dissertation and giving it strength. That's why it should not be used lightly since it's a weapon that can be used for both defense and offense. In both cases, wisdom and knowledge of human nature must be mediators to use this influence in a conscious and necessary way.

There are exercises that can teach you to accomplish

authority with a gaze and reach the mind's domination. In general, these are exercises in which you must hold someone's gaze for a longer and longer period of time without blinking. All of these exercises are necessary, but they require a mind that knows how to focus. That's why, you should learn how to focus on parallel.

A thought that isn't dissociated, meaning, a mind that doesn't divide different small thoughts is what the application of these techniques needs.

When you've exercised and developed the powers of the gaze, you can put them into practice by finding that person in a social gathering who has a weaker character than the person who is applying the technique. These powers will be of great benefit for those who use them in their daily lives. Generally, when someone turns out to be fascinating it is because they're applying the influence of their gaze on everyone else. This influence can be dangerous for those who are weak of character and will be easy victims. A person with a strong character has nothing to fear from those people who try to dominate them because their own nature will protect them and prevent them from falling victim to these tricks.

INFLUENCE THROUGH GOOD EXAMPLE

A thought projected into an enveloping center through a higher influence is received by those brains of weakest caliber, which mechanically register it to reproduce it on similar occasions.

Yoritomo - Tashi

During the civil war, while the great fiefdoms rose in glory, there was a Zen master who lived in a small village. One day, the quiet life they led there was altered by the news that a terrible general was headed there with all his troops to invade those lands. The entire population decided to flee except for the Zen master. When the general arrived, he saw the empty village and heard of this old man who had remained behind. He ordered his men to bring him before him. The old man refused and then, the general walked to the temple in which the old man was, without losing his serenity. The general, drawing his sword, said to him: "Don't you know you stand in front of someone who can pierce you in an instant?" to which the master replied: "Precisely, you are in front of someone who can be pierced in an instant". The general, surprised and confused, after thinking for a moment, bowed and left. This story shows serenity and the courage to stay at peace in the face of adversities. After all, anything can happen at any time.

With this tale as a good example, you can introduce a text, since it predisposes the listener in a good way to the reading. The associations that people can make are related to their own mindset allowing them to influence it consciously or unconsciously.

It's easy to observe how some people seem to absorb others' energies like they're some kind of vampires and that, unintentionally or on purpose, they live at the expense of the people they're absorbing. On the other hand, there are people who seem to irradiate light demonstrating great health and an enormous life that impregnates everything around them. They are cheerful, hold pleasant conversations, other people seek them because they feel contained by them and their words seem to heal them. Other people adopt and put into practice their views, and take their opinion as valid.

In this case, the strongest things seem to be better but it's not always the case. Sometimes: "The influence that individuals exercise on each other is the cause of many evils which are hard to count".[2]

A speaker should be able to influence their audience in a positive way, transmuting negative and selfish thoughts into a series of ideas that seek the common good and altruism. This influence will surely be temporary because at the end of the speech the selfish interests will come back to life and, because they feel safer this way, they will pick up their lives where they left off. The fear of change keeps them still and tied to their customs and criteria. Not all is lost, you can always touch a person whose perspective will change after they hear you. In other cases, new ideas will be left running around in their minds and mature slowly, flourishing when the time is right.

---

[2] *How to Influence People* – Yoritomo, Tashi

It would be positive to question or ask whether it's necessary or correct to suppress the ambition in people, the seed of individualism or to prioritize responsibility to the detriment of altruistic conquests. Current society seems to ask the human being to behave in a certain way, following precepts like: "Time is money", "take care of your image when you go to a job interview" and many more. The economic triumph is put in the foreground and many people worry about it, leaving other matters aside or paying less attention to them.

There was a man who spent large sums of money in a ritual for good fortune. Then, someone asked him: "Wouldn't it be best to light a candle to the saint of prosperity, do the ritual and use the rest of the money to calm poor people's hunger? In this way, the cult of good fortune would be setting a good example and many people with many unmet needs would feel good fortune in their own homes".

Setting a good example is oftentimes more effective than nicely said words.

PLANTING AN IDEA ON PEOPLE'S MINDS

Planting an idea on people's minds can be something beneficial for society as a whole or that can be harmful, depending on the idea.

This technique which is often used by publicists on their adverts leads the reader to direct their thoughts to where they want them to. That's why it must be used carefully and be previously analyzed. It is very powerful and it truly plants an idea on other people. The pattern on which the phrase is developed is the following:

Is (here goes the subject to expose) (a statement about that subject)?

This statement that's made about the subject can be something positive or negative that you expect people to believe or think or notice its existence. The answer to this question can be a simple yes or no, though it's best if it's a rhetorical question that expresses your under covered opinion.

Some examples of these questions are:

- Are vibration platforms the best choice to stay toned at all ages?
- Are vibration platforms too dangerous for those people who have prosthetics and cardiac issues?

With these seemingly harmless and meaningless questions, you're directing the receiver's attention to a belief, or you're simply planting the seed of doubt, or you're widening their knowledge about a subject they didn't know anything about.

In all cases, you're introducing them in a matter that will awaken their intrigue or intellectual curiosity and, maybe, they'll start researching about this subject due to their own restlessness. In this way, they'll analyze the point of view you've exposed in a simple question.

This technique allows for variations in its pattern to create questions and it allows to accomplish new ones that can be just as effective as the previous one.

Some examples of this modifications can be the following questions:

- Have you noticed that…?
- Did you pay attention to…?
- Are you aware of…?
- Have you realized that…?
- Can you understand that…?
- Do you consider that…?
- Have you observed how…?
- Have you ever thought about how…?

And so on, you can continue to list the beginning of phrases which introduce the spectator into a subject. This way, the interrogative sentences will be something like this:

- Have you ever thought about the fact that the image you show others benefits you if it's neat and it aligns to social precepts?
- Are you aware that fuel prices have suffered an unexpected rise in the last fifteen days?
- Do you consider that we must invest in properties that are located in a developing neighborhood?
- Have you realized that if you don't have a resumé that's professionally redacted, it can be more difficult

to find a job?

- Have you noticed the importance of knowing two languages when it comes to getting a well-paid job?

These patterns which have been designed to introduce a subject to the listener have the power to plant an idea in their minds that will develop further on. They can even be used to assess how attentive the listener was to the dissertation on that topic. Both in the middle of it and in the moments where you do a summary before you finish.

For instance, imagine you're trying to sell a book that discusses job performance improvement. In this book, you talk about the importance of flowing with life and the events that come with it. A way of introducing the subject that the book describes would be: Have you noticed that Bruce Lee, a great martial arts artist, used to say: "You have to flow like water because it is soft, it adapts, but it never bends its will"?

In this way you introduce the concept that leads to developing the book you're selling.

APPEALING TO PEOPLE'S IDENTITIES

Every human being has a characteristic identity which differentiates them from the rest. It's their personal stamp. That's why, one of the persuasion methods consists of appealing to their identity and making them notice who they are, who they can become and define who they don't want to be.

In the book *How to win friends and influence people* written by Dale Carnegie, a writer and businessman who developed professionally in human relations and in efficient communications, he states that people must be given a reputation they'll have to maintain and that, surely, they'll make an effort to achieve. There are several ways to accomplish this, one way is through simple and effective sentences which are based in the following pattern:

I can tell that you're a person that (identity) because (you expose the reason why you give them that identity)

For example:

- I can tell that you're a very intelligent person, because you're reading and understanding this book.
- I can tell that you're a person with inner freedom, because you don't seek to fit into any group.
- I can tell that you're a person with high standards, because you've decided to grow and you've come this far.

The word that starts the explanation is a casual connector, since it leads to a certain persuasion even though the reason doesn't make much sense. This is a part of the programming the human being comes with at birth. From a very young age, the reasoning of things is constantly being explained to them. In this way, an identity pattern is generated, and as a corollary, they are given membership in a select group of people that may be wanted by them. Two techniques are combined: on the one hand, the need for identity; and on the other hand, the affiliation need.

A variant of this technique is based on the use of a words' scheme. For example: "Open mind". If you ask a group of people who amongst them are open minded, it's almost certain that ninety percent of the people will claim they do. This way, you guarantee that most people will be in favor of the exposed idea because, if they weren't, it would mean they're close minded.

Some examples which come up as a challenge are:

- How open is your mind to try out the following alternative?
- How open is your mind to give what I'm telling you an opportunity?
- How open is your mind to put this method into practice and enhance your monthly income?
- How open is your mind to allow us to work together?

If you present the options in this way, it's very likely that the person accepts the idea that you're exposing. It's another way of referencing the person's identity. This technique is set on a foundation of consensus in a quick and efficient way. In this foundation, you can then support the later messages that will be persuasive in nature.

It's a technique that is more effective with groups of people who don't know each other than with groups of people who do. You start with an affirmation because when you achieve a first agreement with the listener, it's more difficult that they'll disagree later. That's why, when you explain an idea that can't be summarized in a few words, we tend to use this initial sentence as an introduction. For example:

- I bet you're like me, even just a little bit, and you prefer to have a job that will provide you with great profit in the near future.
- I bet you're like me, even just a little bit, and you hate to waste time in front of the television when you could be doing something productive.
- I bet you're like me, even just a little bit, and you have so many responsibilities that you juggle time so you can fulfill all of your obligations.

Through these affirmations, you'll manage to get to the person and give you the opportunity to elaborate on the ideas you have.

"IMAGINE…"

While someone is talking, the listener forces their mental representations in the direction in which the speech is headed. This is a process that happens naturally as long as there's a transmitter and a recipient.

For instance, if the transmitter says: "While I took a walk, I saw a hawk in a tree that was behind a mill", the audience, unconsciously, will have the mental representation of the tree, the hawk and the mill. If then, he says: "I can't manage to see the hawk, nor the tree, nor the mill because it's foggy", the audience will immediately imagine the fog covering the tree, the hawk and the mill.

In the following sentences, the representations evoked are a bit more complex:

- Understanding this idea is easy.
- Understanding this idea isn't difficult.

Both sentences mean the same thing, but in the listener's mind, varied and abstract representations are displayed. When you begin a speech with words like: imagine that…, think about…; let's suppose that…; etc., you are ordering the mind to use their imagination in the direction we are taking it on.

This process is far simpler if the audience is being talked to about their favorite subjects. When you don't know the audience' s preferences, you can start with the word "Imagine….". It triggers the visualization processes and it allows the audience to recall their preferences, and, in this way, you'll get to know them.

The most descriptive way to understand this, is to pay attention to what happens when you read a book. Written pages become pictures in the reader's mind. Movies or television remove the possibility of letting our imagination run wild because the pictures are already there.

A skillful communicator knows that the key to success is personalizing and humanizing the messages so that they cause, besides the mental representations, the emotions that deeply connect to the message on the listener. The audience will probably forget what they heard, but the way they felt in those moments will be recorded in their involuntary memory.

The advertisements don't sell only a product, they sell the mental representation of what will happen when the consumers buy the product and how it will change their lives. That's why, the best way to deliver a message is through visualization. It's necessary to paint a picture in which the audience feels related to. That's when you must pay the most attention so that the visualization is right, because if it's not appropriate it can play to the product's disadvantage.

For instance, two marketing campaigns where one shows the product in a traditional way and adapts to the consumer's mind, and the other one, which rather not to show direct images but that tries to get the audience to understand the essence of the product itself without a reference. It will be an overstatement to say that the first campaign was truly successful, while the other one was a complete failure.

The first campaign created mental images so that the audience associated the product with them. While in the second campaign, the consumer didn't manage to make a solid assimilation so there was no way to reference the product to any previous image.

The mental images are created in the audience from the stories that you tell them in the adverts. There's nothing more evocative than starting a story with "Once upon a time…", unconsciously, the attention is directed to listening to what's next. However, these words may not be as effective on adults as it is on children, unless it is replaced by: "Imagine that…" This word is like an instruction which predisposes the listener to check their mind for what is being asked to imagine.

This request must contain a benefit and the consequences of not doing what it's being asked of you to imagine. The initial approach must be in a positive way and place the consequences on the background.

"Imagine" is the trigger so that the subconscious starts their image search and the more creative the listener is, the more vivid the images will be, recreating the story with ease. This way, the technique can also be used to request for a raise or a promotion. Generally, people feel intimidated by the thought of coming to their boss's office and requesting a salary raise or a promotion. It's a conversation that requires diplomacy, finesse, as well as determination and strength.

The most relevant thing in this moment is to put yourself in someone else's position, in this case, your boss'. To him, this request means doing a larger investment on the future performance of the person who is requesting the raise. Meaning, the boss won't ask: "What have you done for me lately so that I give you the raise or the promotion?", but rather: "What will you do for me from now on?".

Then, it's necessary to prepare ourselves to explain why our work is good, considering that talking about the past and the current situation won't give an answer to what will happen in the future. That's why, you must mentally organize to tell him about the benefits they will get from agreeing to what you're asking of them. If you've proven your worth to him, you must be subtle when introducing the idea of what the consequences would be if he refuses.

When using the introductory word "imagine if…" you possess an advantage in the situation. For instance, imagine if I hadn't worked on the project you assigned to me, what would have been the outcome? or, imagine if I hadn't been there when you closed the project that provided you this much cost effectiveness, how would you have managed?

In a calm and subtle way, you make your importance known and the consequences he would have suffered without your intervention. In this way, you make them enter a reflective state about your work history. In these circumstances and after the exposition, the boss, if he is intelligent and appreciates you, will give you what you want. Or, on the contrary, he will present reasons why he won't. De esta manera haces que ingrese en un campo de reflexión sobre tu trayectoria laboral.

Another similar pattern is: "How would you feel if…". Here, it's necessary to find an honest and powerful reason to include. You'll also lead him to walk into the realm of potential loss or gain. It is proven that all people worry about losses, so it's more likely that your boss will try to avoid it, than it is that he starts analyzing the potential profit he would have. It's important to find out what is really motivating to him and if he's someone who makes his decisions based on emotions or logic.

HOW TO PLANT DOUBTS AND STOP A "KNOW-ALL"

To have an influence on other people you must learn how to control a conversation or dissertation. Regardless of whether the audience is passive and they just listen or if it's active and participate. Also, you must consider that there can be a "know-all" in the audience who may want to take the audience's attention away from the speaker. Or perhaps, there are people with deep-seated ideas who are more difficult to change their perspective.

That is why it's important to learn how to create a perspective of doubt, an uncertainty that leads to rethinking the foundation of what they believe in. One of the ways to gain back the control of a conversation or dissertation is to go from a perspective of certainty, raised by the person who claims to know it all, to a perspective of doubt, questioning the subject directly, leading them to investigate their beliefs if this certainty is well-grounded.

Like it was explained before, it also happens when the person has deep-seated ideas and it's difficult to make them see a different perspective and incorporate new ideas. This person is convinced that they know so much more than us about the concept on which we're trying to present a different approach. These are people who are difficult to convince, but not impossible.

The best way to go further with the conversation is to

overcome the firm mindset that they have, questioning the knowledge they defended. The goal, from this point forward, is to turn the conversation so that the person ends up admitting that their opinion is based on insufficient evidence. Keeping the interest in the conversation and without losing the thread of the dissertation, doubts are introduced in the following way:

What do you know about...?

This way, you threaten the foundations of the knowledge that you're questioning and, therefore, the person that knows it all begins to draw into the light those references in which they base their arguments. In this way, and without much help, the person will begin to understand that their deep-seated ideas have weak bases and are groundless.

In the following examples you'll clearly see how this situation is managed:

- What do you know about this business and in what way are actions implemented?
- What do you know about the foundations that rise these concepts that I'm presenting today?
- What do you know about the events and occasions that have changed since (here you place the reference)?
- What do you know about the economic and political situation that led to the unravelling of the facts stated today?

- What do you know about the way things work in this place?
- What do you know about the benefits that we're stating in this dissertation?

This way, the person that thinks they are a smart-ass has no choice but to reflect and, like that, they'll arrive at the conclusion that they're reasoning doesn't have a solid ground to support them. By understanding this situation, the person will become more receptive to change. During this whole process, it's necessary to stay calm and never address the person in an aggressive or offensive way, always being respectful and keeping the necessary distance.

The fact of answering with aggressiveness leads the other person to turn defensive and you'll probably get the opposite effect to what you initially wanted to achieve, not only with the subject itself but with the entire audience. The challenge that these kinds of sentences represent lies in the way that they must be used: with confidence, security and coherence, without putting aside the respect that other people deserve even though their views are different and consensus must be achieved through these techniques.

HOW TO CHANGE THE SUBJECT OR THE DIRECTION OF THE CONVERSATION

Changing the subject or the direction of a conversation or dissertation is another one of the skills that a good speaker or lecturer must have. In this technique, you will be changing the direction of the thoughts of those people you are interacting with, leading them in a subtle way to where you want to. This technique is also used to lead the conversation or dissertation from one subject to another. Meaning, when seeing that the person or group are turning an idea over and over again without getting anywhere, the lecturer applies this technique to detour the subject and lead the conversation or dissertation to a convenient place for them.

These types of techniques can be applied to different situations. From everyday life to work life, without skipping all those social opportunities where, at times, it's convenient to change the subject of the conversation being led forward. Imagine how many times you've wanted to change the subject and didn't know how to do it. Remember some moments of your life where this technique could've been used by you as an essential tool and the benefits you would've gained if you had. From now on, every time you face a similar situation, you'll be prepared to overcome the bumps in a conversation.

The way to make this change is through the following linguistic scheme:

The thing isn't (here you introduce the other person's point of view) but (here you introduce your own point of view), immediately after you ask them a question that works as a nexus so you can reach the focus of the subject you're looking for.

For instance:

- The thing aren't the elevated oil prices in middle east, but the bombings in those places where victims are innocent people, even if it's in a faraway place on the planet. What are the measures that governments should take preventively to make peace a reality?
- The thing isn't the insecurity experienced on the suburbs of the city, but the limited possibility to peacefully go out for a walk. How are you working out so that your muscles don't lose their tone?

The subtle way of this language structure, means that there's no need to overanalyze in which way to apply it so that you can achieve a change in the conversation or dissertation. The question about the new subject will be very easy to organize.

Another example that clarifies the ease with which you can use this technique is the following one: Let's assume we're standing in front of a group of businessmen to whom you want to talk to about a seminar which includes a capacitation program in business communication in all the levels of the company.

They are so concerned about their financial problems that they can't stop mulling over the same thing over and over again. Then, you can tell them: "The problem doesn't lie on the results that you'll obtain individually in each of your companies, but in the fact that there is not good communication with your employees, who can't solve problems without adequate advice. What is missing in your work teams so that they can achieve a better performance?

This will lead them to change the focus towards the communication issues between the employees and the hierarchical team who can't achieve the necessary drop in their messages. Clearly the problem boils down to poor communication between both parties. In this way, the conversation will be focused on the communication problems and which would be the possible solutions so that the dialogue flows and is understandable for both parties.

Then, at this point in the conversation you can highlight the need to specialize in the subject and get them to sign up in the seminar that you're trying to promote. The businessmen can start questioning how expensive the seminars are and the great amount of time they require. You can say: "The issue isn't the cost of the seminars, but how much this poor production performance is costing you. If you could appreciate the return of the investment, you're about to make, would you be interested in attending this seminar?".

As you can appreciate, every time the conversation wanted to take an unexpected path, the speaker managed to redirect towards where he really wanted it to go. One thing leads to another and, with some skill, you manage the speech to walk along to our convenience.

THE DTR TRICK TO INFLUENCE

A method that is very effective among the persuasion techniques, is called *"Disrupt - then - Reframe"*, from which its acronym DTR comes from. This technique is considered more of a mind trick than a technique itself. Though it is highly effective and it's important to know it so you can apply it in case that it's necessary, it can be questioned from an ethics point of view, because it is a direct deception to the other person.

The research that gave rise to the DTR technique was made by Davis and Knowles, who in 1999 proved its efficiency by conducting door-to-door sales of greetings cards for the purpose of collaborating with a charity. These sales were preformed using two different techniques:

• First strategy: taking this as a normal reference condition, they told people when they opened their doors that the cost was $ 2,5 dollars for 5 clasps. In this way, they were able to sell in 40% of the visited households.

• Second strategy: taking this as a test DTR condition, they presented the offer to the person who opened the door saying that it cost $ 250 cents for 5 clasps and they immediately added the sentence: "It's a real bargain!" and they were able to sell in 80% of the visited households.

As you can appreciate, the obtained result is far superior in the second case, with just changing the way they presented the offer. What happens in people's minds so that the result is so different from one strategy to the next?

This trick works because it's able to interrupt the ordinary thought and, when the person hears "250 cents", they are left thinking why they say the prize in cents if it can be said in dollars. Then, after this interruption in natural thoughts, comes the restatement with the expression: "It's a real bargain!". This makes the mind of the person spiral down on the prize said in cents and the expression which provides a good quality to the prize, said immediately after.

We must not forget that this whole situation happens in a few seconds, but they're enough to make the person feel confused and accept the fact that the cards are cheap and that it's an opportunity that shouldn't be wasted. If the victim can react and return to their critical thought quickly, then they'll be able to notice the deception and they surely won't fall into it. If they don't react in time, they fall victim to this trick without realizing that it ever happened.

The quicker the salesman is, the less time to think they give the other person and the application if this technique will be successful. If they also add the scarcity technique, saying there are only a few cards available, the effect will boost.

To check that this effect wasn't an isolated case but that it could be applied on different occasions and achieve the expected success, this technique was proved on fourteen later researches which involved hundreds of participants. These studies were conducted by Carpenter & Boster, in 2009. In all of them the obtained results were surprising for the efficiency of this simple technique in which, in comparison, the sales were higher, managed to make people fill the polls and they even managed people to change their attitudes.

In fact, this DTR technique has been effective in those situations of sales in which people often tend to not trust in the salesman's tricks. It's very important to know this strategy, even though, applying or not will be the result of a moral question on behalf of those who use persuasion techniques on a daily basis.

If you find yourself in a situation where you're about to buy something or someone comes to sell you a subscription, it's important that you're prepared so that you won't be fooled by this technique. Consider the possibility that the other person may be trying to use it, therefore, take the time you need so that your thoughts remain critical at all times. Don't let the rush they may display overwhelm you, they are skillful when applying this type of technique and when they see the other person hesitates, they have a new trick under their sleeves.

Interrupting the normal thought flow is a simple fact, but it leaves the person "off service" for an instant, which is very valuable and effective so that the masters of deception can apply these types of machiavellian tricks.

USE OF COMPOUND SUGGESTIONS

Getting other people to accept the suggestions that we make is also a subject of study that will lead you to success. It is possible that you've felt frustrated after having a conversation with someone to whom you gave a great suggestion, but they didn't take it. At that moment you might have thought: " I don't understand why they didn't take my suggestion if it was the convenient thing to do" or "I don't know why they close themselves and run around in circles if I suggested that they open the doors they need".

Despite this, the actual person didn't think of it as something viable. When you try to make someone follow your advice or suggestion, you're trying to persuade them with reasons that might be correct, but that aren't being presented in a way that makes the other person think of them as possible. Perhaps, their mental conditioning is telling them that what you're suggesting isn't the right thing.

The technique that can be used to achieve this result is called: "Use of compound suggestions". This technique is based on the goal of keeping a self-image that is consistent to others, followed by the suggestion we're trying to give. The way to put it into practice is quite simple. You have to say something that is very likely that the other person will agree with and approve of, which means, an accepted truth, and then, you must add the suggestion you want them to take. Seen in a more general way it would be:

Suggestion, opinions or facts that are simply accepted + (what you want the other person to think or do).

To understand it better, let's see the following examples which clarify the concept:

- You get home from work and you rest on your armchair the way you like to. It would be very gratifying to fall into some restful sleep.
- Communication inside the company in an efficient wany and without double messages is fundamental to have a good performance. Your company needs the communication between the different areas to improve in a sustainable way, which is why this seminar is what you need.
- To achieve success in any area of life, it's fundamental to be able to influence and persuade the people you work with. To achieve this goal, it's important to learn and know how to apply an efficient method. This book has explanations, so that you can understand it without any issues.
- To achieve my ideal weight, it's necessary that I do a diet low in calories. This book not only analyzes your calories but it suggests simple exercises that can help you with your weight loss.
- Sympathy and a good presence can help you open those professional doors that you need. A good resume is the endorsement that will build the foundation of the beginning of a work relationship.

At all moments, you must remember besides all that has been stated, the feelings of the group or individual that you're addressing. Most people make their choices based on what they feel and not on what they reason. If when you give a suggestion, you include an evocation to their feelings it will be more effective. You will be creating a hypothetical scene which completes it. In it, the feelings they'll have if they decide to follow your suggestion will be shown.

Making suggestions or giving advice and that other people accept them can be beneficial not only to the person who makes them, but also to the person who takes them. Presenting them considering the feelings will give that suggestion a plus. If you also have the ability to make the person feel no pressure and understand that they are free to make the decision they want, the effectivity will multiply.

THE PATTERN OF: "I AGREE, AND I WOULD LIKE TO ADD THAT…"

This technique explains how you can agree with everything, well still your personal opinion. Knowing how to establish an agreement frame, transforms the person not only into a good persuader, but also into a good mediator that can establish positions which can be understood by both parties.

If you can use this technique along with the redefinition technique in order to modify the direction of other people's thoughts, you'll be in perfect shape to overcome objections who stand in the way and do a complete re-definition of the subject you're dealing with. If you only use this technique, you can get agreements and set conditions which can't be refused. This will be like this, even when the point of view you're incorporating is totally opposite to the one who started the application of the technique.

Be aware that its success will also have to do with sympathy and understanding you achieve with the person. You must remember that the language you use will also be fundamental. Many times, it is believed that speaking lightly will guarantee you success, but it's not like that.

This technique is based on the fact that people enjoy when someone agrees with their ideas and that when someone tells them: "I agree", they are left satisfied. If you see this in yourself, you'll see that if I tell you: "I agree", you'll feel better than if I said: "I disagree".

At this point we must consider that, regardless of whether I agree or not, I will tell you that I agree with you because what I actually think will become irrelevant. This simple sentence: "I agree" will make people keep their defenses down. The fact of saying: "I don't agree", makes the person keep their guard up.

The technique can be started the following way:

I agree and, I'd also like to add that (here you introduce the agreement you'd like to achieve).

Let's see the following example:

- I agree that this seminar has an elevated cost, and I would like to add that regardless of the price: Have you seen how much money you'd make if you applied what you learn from it?
- In the case that the other person says something unpleasant you can reply: "I agree with what you said and I would like to add that only a stupid person would think to say something like that".
- Another possible answer to the previous case would be: "I agree with what you said and I would like to add that there is a perspective different from what you're saying and that could even have better results".

When a person makes a statement, they are revealing what they're thinking and, in many cases, what they're feeling. If you attack it directly, the other person won't listen but they'll prepare to counterattack. When you start the dialogue with an agreement principle, the other person will let their guard down and will prepare to listen to the reasons for which you're saying what you're saying.

By establishing the agreement, you can then use your creativity so that the option that you want to present is taken into account. The speech must be fluid and natural, which is why it's not necessary to say it in a textual way but you can change some words. Instead of saying "I would like to add that" you can say "which means", as you can see in the following examples:

- I agree that it has an elevated cost, which means you're

acquiring a product of better quality.

- I agree that you don't quite understand, which means you still haven't processed all the information.
- I agree that you're in a period of a lot of work, which is why I ask that you reserve some of your time to check the project that I'm presenting to you.
- I agree that this project is important, which is why I'm suggesting you assign it to someone who is able to fulfill it properly.

Finally, this technique is really versatile and it can be easily adapted to what you want to state.

A variant which this technique offers is its possible application in the middle of a dissertation to achieve a little confusion so that the listeners are attentive and don't lose any interest.

A clarification that is worth mentioning, you're probably wondering why is the coordinated conjunction "and" used instead of the adversarial conjunction "but. In these cases, "I agree with you, but..." or "I agree with you, and I would like to add...", make it seem like the second sentence has a greater impact because it adds something to what is being said. On the other hand, the first sentence is overruling what was being said.

THE ILLUSION OF FREE WILL

All human beings have the need to feel that they're free

when choosing or making a decision. No one likes to feel like they're being manipulated or that their ideas are being handled at someone else's will. In psychology, especially on *Ericksonian* hypnosis, there's a technique called "double bond" in which a sentence offers two or more choices that are actually the same one. For instance, it's possible that you can fall into a deep sleep now or within the next couple of minutes.

Besides, there's another technique called: "But you're free to choose". More than forty studies have been conducted which determines that this technique can increase the chances that people accept what you're requesting of them. It consists of making your request and then adding that the person is free to accept or decline. For instance:

- (request), but you're free to decline.
- (request), though, of course, you don't have to do it.
- (request), but it's your choice.

It's important to notice that, regardless of the language you use, what's interesting is that you're giving them a choice. This technique is more effective when you have the other person right in front of you. This doesn't mean that it can't be effective in distance, meaning, via telephone, e-mail, or social media.

There's a variation of this technique in case that the person knows their options and needs help to make a choice. In this case, the sentence would be:

The way I see it, you have (x) options.

Apparently, you're only telling them what their options are, but you can show them in a way that the final choice is in your favor. This can be accomplished by putting the option you prefer last, highlighting it as a favorite. If you're starting a business and you need someone to join your idea. You've found the right person, but you have to convince them. So, you present them with a scene in which you highlight the option you want them to choose.

The scene can be the following: "Is it true that you're not convinced by your current job? You have to work long shifts, you're left with little time to spend with your family and the payment is not as much as you'd expected. I present you with this opportunity that, as you've said, seems like a good one though you're scared of change. The way I see it, you have three choices: first, you find another job with all that it implies, filling out the requests, doing the interviews, working during a non-remuncrated period, etc., second, you stay on your current job, accepting it as it is and, third, you can try what I'm offering you, parallel to your current job and see how it works out for you. What do you think it's best for you?".

Ending the presentation with a question means that you're free to choose. Besides, the option you want them to choose is presented as something simple and easy to carry out. Definitely, your goal is to become a catalyst of options where you expect they choose the one you present better and always in the last place.

When you present options, the more polarized they are, the easier they'll choose.

For example:

- Generally, you can say that there's two types of people: those who leave their financial success up to their employees' actions or those who take the wheel for themselves and build their own company. Which kind of person are you?
- Generally, you can say that there's two types of people: those who make their judgement without trying something out, and those who try it and then base their opinions on the lived experience. Which kind of person are you?
- Generally, you can say that there's two types of people: those who don't accept change, thinking that all things from the past are better, and those who adapt to the running of time, creating a better future. Which kind of person are you?

A variant of this technique is the "decoy effect". In it, the situation is described, providing three choices from which two are legitimate and the third one, which is semi-legitimate, is a decoy. For instance: three options for a web's subscription. In the first one, the price is $ 59 dollars a year. In the second one (printed version, it's $ 125 a year and the third one is the printed and online subscription for $ 125 dollars a year.

The second choice is a decoy because for the same

price you can get the third option, which includes the web version and the printed version. As you can see, depending on how you present the options, you'll accomplish the success you're looking for.

LIE BY COMMISSION, LIE BY OMISSION AND DENIAL

Being able to realize when someone is trying to manipulate you, is a skill that favors survival in today's society. Every single person in the environment you develop in has their own interests and it's important to be able to determine in which measure those interests can harm you.

Manipulative people have years of practice in machiavellian psychology and in many varied and good techniques, besides having traits that characterize them and which can identify them. One of the most typical traits is the fact of lying. You can lie by omission or by omission. By commission is what is known as the classic lie, you're simply saying something that isn't true. It's a deliberate action whose goal is to deceive or confuse gaining some benefit from it. Generally, this type of lies is made with the intention to get out of trouble or because explaining the truth will take time and effort. It may not be told with bad intentions, but it's still a lie.

A manipulator is known for lying all the time, because it's so ingrained that telling the truth is not a part of their customs.

The lie by omission is also known as "exclusive details". In this case, they tell a portion of the truth but exclude certain details on purpose. These lies are slightly more sophisticated than the previous ones. The person who tells them can come up victorious in the event that they get caught. Even if it's a legal situation, they walk free for the fact that they can plead that the person who asked them wasn't specific enough about the details they had to tell.

The clearest example of these kinds of lies is when a salesman talks about a product's benefits, without mentioning the negative aspects that come with using it. Another example would be: when a person makes three comments about you, one is criticism and the other two speak favorably of you. Someone tells you about it and if that person is even, they'll mention the three comments, but if it's a manipulator and there's the choice to get an advantage from that comment, they'll only tell you about the criticism and not mention the positive comments.

Not correcting the concept mistakes that other people make when you hear them talking is also a form of lie by omission. With these types of lies you can take other's guesses to a convenient point. A skillful manipulator will know how to use this resource.

For instance, a person dressed as a policeman outside a bank, those who see them assume, without asking, that they are guarding the bank, even if they went there for personal reasons. The context that the observer sees, makes their mind reach a conclusion which seems logical, even if it might not be true. Manipulators know these types of tricks and, of course, they use them to their favor.

Another aspect which is used by manipulators is denial. Denial means that a person can't accept reality for some reason. The masters of deception take advantage of denial to feign innocence when they know, perfectly well, what they've done. They use it to control what other people think or the interpretations they make of a certain event.

In some cases, they're able to make a person question themselves. This is a very subtle mental abuse and it can be hard to detect sometimes. When you confront a manipulator, they will use denial to carry on. However, you must differentiate whether the manipulator is conscious of what they are doing or if they actually believe in their own lie. If it's the second case, you stand in front of a person who struggles with some form of mental illness.

Denial can be used as a defense mechanism, as a manipulation tactic, or it can be used to avoid taking some kind of responsibility. In every case, it's a way of causing serious psychological damage to the victims, which means that if any person in your environment uses it, it's convenient you take care of yourself.

RATIONALIZATION AND MINIMIZATION

The rationalization of an event means giving a reasonable frame to what is being said or to a determined event. It's also a way of creating excuses. The people who use manipulation have the ability to create a reasonable version that justifies their behavior.

Even when everyone condemns them, the manipulator will find a way to find the perfect rationalization to their actions. In these excuses, they'll shape the way you perceive them and they might even make you change your mind. It can be used as a defense mechanism so that the actions seem ethically acceptable and morally reasonable.

When someone tries to rationalize concepts that are wrong, you must test what they're saying to know they're feeling about that subject. Even if the conversation is about something hypothetical, you can learn a lot about the feelings they have about the subject of the conversation.

In these cases, it's important to keep in mind that, if a person close to you justifies something in your presence and you don't express your disagreement in what they're saying, they'll understand that you agree with their perspective. In their mind, this implicit agreement that came up from your silence will be recorded, and will possibly be used on a future occasion. Which means, this seemingly meaningless thing can lead the person to rationalize that you agree with more important concepts that are related to that subject that you, supposedly, agreed with.

When it comes to minimization, the psychological action that it triggers can have unexpected consequences. Minimization consists of taking importance away from the emotions or actions that a person has or makes, with the intention of manipulating them or lowering their self-esteem. Parents, for instance, tend to minimize their children's anger because they seem exaggerated for the adult mind even if they're really important for the child.

A manipulative person uses rationalization and minimization in conjunction or one after the other. For instance, when a determined situation can't be properly rationalized, the manipulator will try to minimize it to put it in an exaggerated context on the other person's hand. When you accomplish any significant achievement in your life, there will always be a manipulative person who will try to minimize it to make other people see that your accomplishment is not that transcendental. A narcissistic person will try to make your accomplishment be considered as team work, minimizing your contribution in it.

In a couple, it can happen that one of them minimizes the other's feelings, making them seem insignificant. Another common thing in these relationships is that the man complains about how exaggerated the woman is and how she makes a drama out of meaningless things. A woman could say that the man is unmanly because they openly express their emotions. This way of acting towards others can make the person who receives the minimization feel self-conscious, frustrated and, in some cases, belittled and put aside.

Those who exercise abuse on other people, whether it's physical or psychological, will use minimization to justify that their actions aren't harmful as the victim claims. In these cases, the abuser hints that it could have been much worse and, in most cases, the victim begins to think that the abuser is right and that, luckily, they know how to control themselves so there weren't worse consequences.

Another way of using minimization is through what is known as cognitive distortion. In some cases, certain actions or emotions are distorted so that they seem less important. A characteristic example of this is: when a person insults another one and, when confrontation happens thanks to the attacked person, the aggressor claims it was only a meaningless joke and that they should get a sense of humor.

This use of minimization is found in every order of life, whether in the personal one, or the professional one, aside from being used by the institutions. It's necessary to be careful of those people who minimize others because they tend to cause a lot of harm.

THE REFLECTION

There are people who have the ability to understand each and every one of the feelings or attitudes of others. Like they can read what the other person is going through like it was a book. This ability means that those who have it can act like a chameleon and transform into the other person. They will see themselves reflected on them, as if they were looking at a mirror. This reflection will include tastes, preferences and current or past situations. They will match on every level of existence.

The people who learn how to read personalities follow a technique which divides itself in three levels. In these three levels, they recollect the information that will allow them to create the reflection.

In the first level they recollect information through third parties who know the person, whether through work, friendship, etc., getting information like their address, where they work, the school they went to and all those things that are fundamental aspects of the life of the target that is being researched.

Then, they search information online in social media and in depth. People have the custom to show their lives in social media and that makes it easier to obtain information about them. For instance, if all the pictures they post are at a specific bar, on a first date the researcher can take their victim there and they will feel impressed with the coincidence.

In the second level, the first conversations start, which will be all about the victim so that they open their hearts and turn confident. By having the information obtained in the first level, this will be the entryway so that the victim explains their deepest subjects, such as their feelings, their first loves and what made them fall in love, their disappointments, their family problems, their work life, etc. The person who is investigating will attentively listen, as if they're feeling any kind of empathy, but it's actually a mask.

In fact, after every date, when they're alone, they'll write down all the information in a notebook so they don't forget anything. It's a cold and calculated research.

In the third level, they go even deeper with the investigation. The person goes further with their idea of probing. For instance, they talk of a specific food dish and observe if the corner of the mouth of the victim goes upward or downward. If it goes downward, they change the subject and mention a different dish. This procedure is repeated until they find the dish that the victim truly loves. This information will also go to their notebook.

Then, in a letter conversation, they will use these facts to start talking about themselves. This way, they unravel every subject of the other person's lives, appreciating their body language and not letting a single detail slip through. They pay attention to the dilation of their pupils, what they do with their hands, the tone of their voice and in which moment of the conversation they turn passionate, and in this way, the notebook progressively becomes a book of the victim's life.

At this point, they use the information to show the victim that they are very pleased with them, that there are many coincidences between their tastes, evidencing that there's a great connection between them and that it seems as if they've known each other for a long time. This feeling that they've started "a long time ago" accelerates the relationship that is, in fact, premature. But the feeling of safety and contempt that this kind of machiavellian person offers makes the victim fully trust them. It is possible that at this point of the relationship you hear sentences such as: "You're my other half", "you're the person that completes me", etc.

Most people look for a soulmate and this scamming person fulfills the fantasy of becoming the victim's soulmate. The more need for affection the person has, the easier it will be for the manipulator to get what they want.

This is how the scammer becomes the reflection of the victim. Every time they see the person, they won't be able to help seeing themselves and in this way the desire for their victimizer will increase, and the fear of losing this idyllic thing which presented itself unexpectedly and which seems perfect in every way will also grow.

The illusion created around this relationship will wrap the victim up in a fictional reality where they'll be controlled if they don't manage to react in time and understand what is truly happening, and they'll end up being truly harmed once the victimizer achieves their goals.

EVASION

Evasion is a technique that favors the manipulator. Through it, they can distract people's attention and draw it away so they don't notice the behavior they're displaying at that moment. This way, by drawing attention to a different focus, they can avoid being exposed and keep their true intentions hidden. Other people, if they're not aware of their manipulation, won't notice their actions and the manipulator will avoid taking the responsibility they should take for the actions they're performing.

Making use of evasion is generating a rambling environment in which irrelevant comments are abundant when reality demands a specific answer. When the manipulator receives a direct question, which will put them in evidence, they start giving a speech that tangentially addresses the subject, but they have the ability to avoid it with details that have nothing to do with the question itself.

The person who uses evasion, will never give a direct and concrete answer to the question they are being asked. Deviation often goes after the evasion because, subtly, they change the subject and go somewhere else, leaving the manipulator free of guilt and blame. When you use deviation, you direct attention to a different subject that, in order to be more effective, must cause indignation. This way, people forget about the previous subject and, once again, the manipulator walks away from answering a question that would have framed them.

The most typical case of evasion is when a person asks their child where they went for the school's field trip. The child starts talking of the problems they faced in math or what the history teacher told them, perhaps they'll tell some gossip that involves other students and, in this way, they manage to make the person forget what they asked. When a manipulator sets a situation in which they use deviation, they'll generally return to an unresolved subject and, if this subject has previously led to an argument, they'll use it with more reason.

Evasion, along with deviation are commonly used by politicians in the interviews that give when the journalist tries to discuss a problem that isn't solved. They would also use the technique of anger, directing the focus to a subject that causes the listeners' outrage. If the previous subject also caused indignation, the new subject has to be ostentatiously more sensitive to the audience.

Needless to say, these techniques are also used by the companies' managers who deal with Public Relations, also by lawyers who try to avoid the exposure of their clients to general opinion.

In those cases in which these techniques don't work out because the person who's asking doesn't detour from their purpose of getting a concrete answer, the manipulators can try to use other techniques. The most common one is praising people, telling them they're so smart that explaining it to them would be a way to treat them as if they weren't.

We mustn't forget the fact that evasion in conjunction -or not- with deviation, hides a deception. The manipulator is trying to keep something from reaching the spotlight, because if it did, they'll be harmed.

GASLIGHTING

This is a truly dangerous technique for the victim. It consists of making the person doubt and question their own reality. Which means they doubt their own lives, what they perceive, their memories, what's in their past and, in this way, they start believing what the manipulator is telling them.

In these cases, the manipulator will start planting doubts so that they start thinking they're misremembering things, that they're going crazy or getting sick. The victim will start using denial in the facts that are real, they will feel disoriented, they'll enter contradiction and their entire world will begin to fall apart. If the person continues to be subjected to *gaslighting* for long periods of time they'll turn unstable, even becoming a danger to themselves.

For instance, when you tell a person that they never properly remember what happens and they are subjected to such psychological violence that they start not paying attention to what goes on around them because they'll remember it wrong anyways. An abuser using this technique can make the person believe that the abuse never took place. These kinds of manipulations work because you never see it coming. The first steps the manipulator takes are with small lies to prove how feasible it would be to carry on with the *gaslighting*.

For example, the fact of making the other person think they're exaggerating everything. At the beginning, they'll start saying it about something small and they'll convince them it's that way. Then they'll use the same idea on something far more transcendental and this person will think that they're right since it has previously been proven to be like that, and that way, the manipulator will be able to make them believe that all their expressions are truly exaggerated. This way, it is evident that the work performed by the manipulator is subtle, detailed and constant, which leads the person to believe that their mental health is deteriorating and that their reality is blurring out.

This technique is more effective when the person who applies it is in a position of power over the victim, for instance, a boss, a person who economically sustains another one, a spiritual leader, etc.

A form in which the victimizer applies *gaslighting* is by refusing to listen to what the victim has to say or making them believe that they don't understand what they're saying. This technique is known as "retention". Another form is the explained one, where the manipulator puts into question the victim's memory. This way is known as "counteract". First, they put it into question and then they say: "What happened was…" and they give their version of the facts. It's possible that in that version the manipulator is a hero, the one who saved the day, or they might even show themselves as a victim who sacrifices for others. Another form they use are minimization, deviation and even blocking. They can get to say phrases such as: "The situation is already bad enough without you exaggerating it".

A way to uncover them is paying attention to these kinds of answers. As small as they seem, they're like a red flag that goes off and warns us to pay more attention.

PROJECTION

This technique manifests when the manipulator projects

their emotions and problems on the victim. The person who acts this way, generally, is someone who doesn't know how to handle their own feelings, they get easily stressed out and the act of projecting gives them back some inner peace to overcome the situation they're going through.

It can be considered as a defense mechanism that, in most cases, can be harmless since it is a part of human nature to project negative thoughts on the people who surround them.

It is harmless to a certain degree, but it can become a dangerous manipulation technique if it's combined with one of the previous ones. For these types of people, it's nearly impossible to recognize that their actions have consequences. It's easier to blame others and avoid taking responsibility for what they've done.

For instance:

- A person who systematically lies, can tell their partner that they're lying because they're left with no choice.
- A person with compulsive behavior will always transfer their problems to others because it's too difficult for them to recognize that they're sick.
- A beating person, when hitting someone else and harming their fist will say: "I had to go to the doctor to get my hand checked because of you".
- A grandmother that tells her grandson to be good or else the lady will get mad. The lady is a strange person to what is happening, but the grandmother transfers to her the fact that she's not able to challenge her

grandson.

A person who likes to manipulate is someone who we might call machiavellian. They want to exercise control over the people who surround them. Definitely, they're very insecure with themselves and they seek, elsewhere, the safety they should have within them.

When a boss, a partner, a father or a son ask for explanations and lead, through their speech, the other person is obliged to reply. The victim allows themselves to be dominated because their feelings tell them they aren't delivering to the other person, meaning, they feel guilty in a way and they need to make it up.

Projection is such a natural thing that children use it without even knowing what they're doing. It's common that when you confront a child for what he's done, he says: "Juan did it", being that Juan is his name but he puts the blame outside of himself because in this way they release the tension that being guilty causes in them. Or else, they blame an imaginary friend. It's very common that this happens when the child wets themselves.

Sometimes, the victim feels compassion for their victimizer and projects their feelings of solidarity and empathy in them. In these moments, they'll try to convince them but the altruistic feelings they deploy on the other person play against them and the manipulator will gain an easier victory. In this case, a double projection is generated.

The manipulation that is exercised through projection isn't always detected. When the victim realizes that this is happening, it's convenient that they directly speak with their victimizer and try to rationalize what they're going through, putting aside the emotions that might come up which won't be beneficial to the rationalization that you're trying to achieve.

ISOLATION

The human being is a social being who needs the support from the people who surround them. When someone is going through a stressful situation or a difficult process, these people will support them and help them move on. The manipulator knows this need, which is why, to gain the control they're looking for, they'll try their best to isolate the victim. The people who are alone or those who were separated from their loved ones can easily fall into the abuse and control of a manipulator.

For instance, those who are self-proclaimed leaders in some religious cults do their indoctrination emphasizing on how sick society is which is why it's convenient to stay on its sideline and relate only to the people who belong to the cult. This is the way in which they act, planting mistrust and emphasizing the small conflicts that can exist. Slowly, they manage to separate the person from their surroundings.

In a work environment, they'll observe relationships and create enemies by highlighting the small conflicts that already exist. They're deception professionals, which is why they succeed. They're able to defame and discredit someone with the purpose of isolating them from their surroundings, applying the machiavellian concept: "Divide and you shall conquer".

After achieving the isolation of the victim, the manipulator uses another technique such as *gaslighting,* seeking control of their lives. Another way in which they can control is isolating them with the purpose of punishing them, which means, the manipulator organizes a gathering and invites the whole work group except for the victim, but they make sure that they find out so that they feel separated from the group.

In the case of couples' relationships there's a very efficient technique before applying the isolation technique and controlling the other person's life. It's interesting to learn it so that you can be prepared in case you face a manipulator who uses it. With this technique they earn the victim's trust because they confuse their senses and encourage them to act recklessly and without rationally analyzing their behavior. Besides, as a secondary effect, the victim finds themselves wrapped up in:

- An excess of love which will later be restricted.
- So much trust that their defenses will be completely inactive.
- An idyllic time which will be remembered later.
- Such competent that they'll open their heart telling all of their life's details. Information which will later be used against them.
- Being highlighted as someone special and being taken into account.

In this way, they prepare the ground to introduce another technique and fully control the victim, like, for instance, the reflection technique. This method started in the Unification Church in the United States and was called: "Love bombing" (*Moonies*) in the '70s. It was a way of acting towards newcomers in which the stable members filled the new members with affection, making them feel as if they were part of the family. [3]

This love bombing is a real avalanche of affection that can make the other person feel like they're in debt with the person who applies this technique. It's very difficult to escape these waves, so much apparent "contempt" and so many considerations that feed a person's sensitivity. In a later stage, this person will introduce their friends who will also enlarge the victim, making a more than pleasant environment. They can also give them poems, flowers, songs that speak of both of them, etc.

This method makes everything happen in a vertiginous way, which is why it doesn't allow for time to think, it creates a deceiving reality, a solid relationship apparently premature is formed and the illusion of a "*happy ever after*" is created. What is being experienced isn't questioned at any moment (we'll return to this in detail in a later chapter.

If a person tries to warn the victim and tell them they are being manipulated, the victimizer will minimize the accusation stating that: "They're jealous of the beautiful relation-

---

[3] Manipulation - H. G. Tudor

ship they have" or "they're meddling into something that doesn't concern them and they're talking of things they do not know because only we understand our relationship" which will contribute to a greater isolation.

Finally, being isolated, there are no people left around the victim who can tell them what their manipulator is doing. They live in a fictional reality created from the attention they receive where this controlling person is their entire world, also considering that everything they say is some sort of sacred law. We must remember that at this point, the victim will be afraid of losing this relationship and be left completely on their own.

BRINGING UP THE PAST

> *I like to use two words in particular when I'm bringing up the past. You'd better pay attention to these words since they're key indicators that I'm applying this manipulation technique. These two words are "always" and "never". In this way, I remind you of that one thing you used to do in the past and that you're no longer doing.*
> H. G. Tudor

Bringing up the past is a technique that is commonly used by people who try to manipulate the present. The past, generally, is filled with guilt, of things that could have been done but that weren't, of feelings that could have been expressed but that remained secret, of choices that could have been made but that we weren't brave enough to make.

Manipulators research their victims and find out the secrets they keep in their past, treasuring them to bring them to the light when the occasion calls for it. Their experts in the art of handling the feelings evoked by the past.

Sometimes, it seems incredible that a person who barely remembers what happened yesterday, suddenly recalls details of an event that happened years ago like they were watching it happen as in a movie. This is how selective memory can be when you associate it to both positive and negative feelings. Even more so, if the person has the intention of manipulating another with the events that take place.

The memories associated to positive feelings make up the memory which comforts the person, on the other hand, the memories associated to negative feelings make up that memory which can torment and their emotional aspect. This aspect is one of the points which are used by the manipulator to control their victim.

You mustn't forget the fact that these torments can be overcome and truly, be left in the past. In this case, the manipulator won't be able to use them because the person was able to overcome them. When the manipulator brings up the past, they do it because they expect that the other person gets emotionally unstable or remembers bad feelings which will depress them. For instance, some of the memories that can be conflicting for a person are:

- Remembering that they wet the bed as children. This memory can make them feel defenseless.
- Not passing a test that left them out of a job. This

memory will make them feel as if they missed out on a great opportunity.

- Being excited over moving out to a different city or country, but when the opportunity presented itself, they didn't have the guts to do it. It's likely that this memory can make them feel frustrated for what could have been in their lives.
- Not expressing how they felt on time and having a love get away which was very significant to the person. This memory, probably, will make them feel as if they lost the love of their lives.

The fact that the manipulator selects these kinds of memories which move feelings and that are, of course, unresolved subjects for the victim, leads them to unbalance. Then, the victimizer will comfort their victim, minimizing feelings and making them feel small and, therefore, subdued. In this position, they will be easy to manipulate.

Sometimes this resource of bringing up the past is used to avoid giving explanations of actions performed by the manipulator. For instance, someone receives a suspicious message on their phone and their partner notices a strange behavior and asks them for explanations. Then, this person who was caught *in fraganti* replies with an allusion to their past, deviating the attention from the text they received.

It's common to act this way when someone is trying to cover up an infidelity. It's likely that they'll also make their partner feel so guilty that they won't want to go out with them in public so they don't make them have a bad time.

Which will make them have a free way to carry on with their infidelity.

The victim, who believes what their victimizer tells them, gives them a free pass because they're too afraid of losing them, since they made them see that relationships can be fragile and easily damaged. At this point, the manipulator will pretend to be offended and to be having a hard time forgiving their partner, making them notice that they should take better care of the relationship. In some cases, they'll use threats to have better effectiveness.

For instance, the most frequent way to complain about something bringing up the past is:

- I always find the mugs dirty, why don't you wash your mug after you use it? Is it only my job?
- You never go out with me, you prefer your friends, you used to prefer going out with me.

The past is an archive that a manipulator who knows their victims can go to. Which is why it's important to work on the traumas that might've come up due to certain experiences, so you can overcome them and stop them from being used against you.

SHAME AND DEFAME

Shame, also called humiliation, is a feeling that makes a person feel uncomfortable and exposed. In that moment, you grow aware of a behavior that might've been exaggerated, wrong, inappropriate or silly. Since it's a feeling that comes from a behavior, and the behavior has to do with the social norms of the society we live in, we can say that shame is a feeling that results from a social construct and that is, therefore, determined by subjectivity.

For example, when you go to the beach and you get in the sea an inopportune wave removes the top part of your bathing suit. If this ever happened to you, you know that in that moment you couldn't find the best way to cover yourself up. However, there are nudist beaches where this situation would be meaningless. Another example is to be ashamed of being an overweight person in a culture that glorifies thinness. In other times, an overweight body was a synonym of beauty.

The manipulator often gives belittling nicknames so the victim feels ashamed, since these nicknames ridicule a body part or a trait in their character. Another way in which they can shame them, is to make fun of every opinion they express and minimize their ideas.

This effect is accentuated when the person who's embarrassing them is in a position of power. It doesn't necessarily have to be a boss; it can also be a person whose opinion is incredibly valued by the victim.

This feeling will make you vulnerable in front of other people, because society demands certain behaviors, attitudes, idioms, etc., and if they're not met, they cause shame as a self-demanding response for not achieving the standards that were set. Only balanced people in this regard can understand that not following social norms isn't always shameful.

Which is why, if by any reason you don't feel shame, the manipulator will make sure that you do by using all kinds of tricks, like bringing to your attention that this, or that person, was scandalized by something you said or did. This shame leads the person to adjust their behavior according to social norms. It is often used on children to correct their attitudes.

Shame will be used by a narcissistic person to prove that they're superior to you. A sadist will use it because they enjoy the moment when you're flustered and a machiavellian person will use it so you act according to their will.

The manipulator, after shaming their victim, tries to defame them, thus accomplishing their total disavowal on a social level. The victim can come out from this situation looking really bad. It can happen in two ways: Convincing others that the victim is a fraud or an aggressor and taking their social and professional prestige away, or convincing the victim themselves that their own actions are fraudulent or aggressive.

Needless to say, the manipulator will use a combination of techniques to achieve their goals: rationalization, minimization, *gaslighting*, etc. By all means they'll try to make the victim look like a victimizer. For instance, when a couple ends their engagement, it's usual that one of them talks badly of the other with other people making them seem guilty of the breakup.

Another thing the manipulator tries to achieve is convincing others that their behavior was caused by a provocation made by the other person, and that whatever they did, the victim deserved it. The victimizer knows very well what they're doing with their victim, but it's best for them if people think that they're right because it's their way to not only control their prey but also their surroundings. In this way they'll show, or at least that's what they think, that the victim is at their feet and that their superiority is unquestionable.

Also, in this way, the most gruesome crimes and most perverse abuses have happened. When the manipulator feels they're in total control of the situation they also believe they can do as they please with their victim.

The motifs that move a manipulator can be many. One of them is envy and the desire to connect with the world in the way the chosen victim does. The defamation they put into motion attacks every aspect of this person's life, being wrapped up in a vortex of things they can hardly understand how they happened.

Defamation is a terrible action that has unexpected consequences. Depending on how bad the defamation is, the person could easily overcome it or struggle with its consequences for a long time.

POSITIVE REINFORCEMENT

Positive reinforcement is a way to acknowledge someone else's actions and, in a way, reward them. It's a kind of award for doing a good job for performing a good deed. It's been proven that when you put it into practice, there are more chances that good behavior or actions will be repeated.

All human beings like to be recognized for their efforts because it means that what they have been doing wasn't useless but that, in being recognized, it made a difference between the fact of doing nothing and taking action in this matter. Religious people believe that they have to be good to others so that God rewards them in heaven. Religious leaders also add that, if you misbehave, God will punish you. It is also used in children as a way to make them set apart what is right from what it isn't. For instance:

- You earned this candy because you put your toys away.
- Today you choose the movie we're going to watch because you cleaned your bedroom.
- I'll buy you dinner for making me look good in front of the boss.
- Today you don't have homework because you did the science homework in such a short amount of time.
- This month you'll get an extra bonus for the increase in productivity you've achieved.

Generally, positive reinforcement is used so that the person understands that their actions resulted in benefits that are appreciated. However, manipulators also use it as a way to handle their victims and keep them under their control. In this case, positive reinforcement will be something that will play against the person.

The mind, in general, takes this reinforcement as a consequence of what they've done. This can be observed in trained animals: after they do their tricks they are rewarded with a treat. They can connect their trainer's instructions with what they have to do and the prize they receive at the end. The human being's mind also makes that connection between what they do and what they get in return. Then, when they do it again, they'll be waiting for their reward. For example: the children who eat their vegetables and get a delicious ice cream for dessert. Every time they eat vegetables, they'll be waiting for ice cream.

The adult may or may not wait for the reward they received for certain actions, but what they will remember is what they felt when their efforts were acknowledged and those feelings will motivate them to perform new actions.

Those who try to manipulate will look for the reinforcement that causes behaviors which benefit them or that will make the victim forget about their own actions. In that case, the message they're giving is: "If you don't criticize what I'm doing, you'll get a reward you like". For example, a boss who gives gifts to an employee so they don't say that he's diverting the company's funds to his personal account. Another example would be when you pay a significant sum of money to a public functionary so that they approve your projects quicker.

The manipulator is able to go far with these kinds of tricks in order to achieve what they've set their minds to. They can even give a very important reward so that the person performs a specific action against their will. This is also related to the moral values the victim has, if they're a person strong in their convictions, as much as they're offered something, they wouldn't agree to being involved in questionable actions.

Anyways, the manipulator will try to numb their senses with these reinforcements which, at the beginning, will be small, but since they are capable of accepting them, they will attempt something far greater in exchange of a more relevant action next time. This way, their requests will keep growing and, of course, so will their rewards.

Surely, the first reward they'll use will be a public acknowledgment to show others that they're truly grateful for the performed actions. This will be the starting point so that the victim thinks they're important in their victimizer's life. It is possible that this acknowledgment makes their relationship stronger and the victim will be more trusting of them. The development of this trust will also make them lower their guard and make them see the following rewards as normal, even if they're not, because within them, they feel like there's a friendship that binds them together.

Some people have the custom to start a conversation by stating how intelligent you are or how able you are to solve problems, before asking you to do something for them. It's up to you to do them the favor they ask or letting them know that you realize the manipulation they're trying to use on you.

NEGATIVE REINFORCEMENT AND PUNISHMENT

Just like the positive reinforcement after an expected action is used, there also exists the negative reinforcement, in which a fact which is considered harmful is avoided by performing an action that someone needs or expects you to do. It's a little different to punishment, since in this case, a negative fact is applied when you don't act the way the other person expects you to.

This model is also used by manipulators to push their victims so that they do what they want. At times, they use punishment, if it's convenient to them, but the negative reinforcement puts more psychological pressure on them. Punishment is a concrete fact that can be more or less painful, but negative reinforcement acts on their mind and emotions, creating a fantasy about what could happen if they don't fulfill what is being asked of them.

For example:

- Wash the dishes if you don't want to find them full of ants tomorrow.
- Brush your teeth if you don't want to get cavities.
- Fill the taxes form if you don't want to get a ticket.
- Start being more productive If you don't want to lose this job.
- No person is essential so make an effort to make a difference.

- Don't eat sugar if you don't want to get fat.
- Train every day if you don't want to lose the competition.
- Update your knowledge if you don't want your employees to know more than you do.
- Get the surgery if you don't want your husband to cheat on you or leave you.
- Make an effort to get that raise if you don't want your wife to be disappointed in you.
- If you get good grades, you'll save yourself from cleaning up your room.
- If you pay attention in class, I won't make a quiz tomorrow.

As you can see, negative reinforcements are present in every aspect of life and they're more common than you'd expect. They're applied hoping to strengthen the requested responses, punishment, on the other hand, debilitates the responses because the person starts getting unmotivated and worn out. Therefore, the manipulator will use one or the other depending on what's convenient for them.

It's possible that when you think of negative reinforcements the following question comes up: "Why is it called negative if it results in a positive behavior?", meaning, if someone quite smoking thinking they won't get cancer that way, can be analyzed as positive or healthy. The act itself (quitting smoking) is positive, but it was done thinking about the fear of cancer, instead of thinking about gaining health. That's the reason why it's called negative.

The word negative doesn't mean that the objective to accomplish is actually negative, but that it's being done for the wrong reasons, meaning, moved by fear. It's used to promote certain actions but it's possible that it triggers some problematic behaviors. The person receiving this psychological action will start putting away their own frustrations and anger which will come out eventually with consequences that can't be foreseen.

Generally, negative reinforcement works when the person does what they're being asked because they want to stop that negative stimulus that's haunting them. However, in the case of punishment, the person acts trying to avoid negative actions being done to them. Actions that can paralyze them and turn them into a puppet.

The negative reinforcements create a stressful environment in every aspect of life. In the home aspect, it will generate mistrust in all the members of the family, and in the work aspect, it will create an unhealthy competition among employees, aside from applying the "every man for himself" instead of generating companionship. This environment will also be detrimental to the employees' morale, destroying work teams, increasing the conflicts, mistrust and the consequences of these emotions will be clear in the middle and long-term, though initially, it might seem like a solution for a specific problem.

Disciplinary sanctions in school areas are also an example of negative reinforcement. The pressure exerted by the big nations who achieved development over those who couldn't accomplish the same level of development is also an example of negative reinforcement and of subduing over the fear of the consequences.

In the case of the transit tickets, we can also talk of negative reinforcement. But that reinforcement avoids those malicious actions which will harm the members of a society are performed, therefore, they're based on the common good and it's been more than proven that they're necessary. The same thing happens with the legislations that govern the different countries, they're thought out for the harmonious development of society, though it may seem a negative reinforcement.

In recapitulation, every time someone requests an action and they insist so that it is performed or else this or that will happen, they're applying the negative reinforcement technique.

PERSISTENCE

Persistence is an interaction in which
a person makes a repeated request
while the other one ignores that request repeatedly
and both of them get upset
as the battle of wills intensifies.
Alejandro Mendoza

To persist is, from some points of view, a positive fact since it invites to not give up in the face of adversities and to stay focused on a goal. Though, it also has a negative aspect and it can be used as a manipulation technique. Persistence is one of the most common ways the human being has to communicate. Within certain limits, it's healthy and harmless. It's a battle of intentions between two or more people that, as long as it doesn't violate any rights, has no further consequences beyond the difference in interests.

Persisting is to insist to a point in which you upset or intimidate the other person. It's constantly reminding the person, in a subtle or obvious way, that they do something they don't want to do for whatever reasons, or that they were planning on doing later.

For instance:

- I won't leave here until you change your clothes.
- Quit smoking or else I'll keep reminding you to do it
- Start your diet already so I don't have to keep listening to you complaining about how clothes don't fit you.

Parents use it all the time with their children because they seem to be fixated in only executing their will. Managing to establish habits in favor of their health requires the parents' persistence. Sometimes, getting them to study is also the result of the insistence of parents, teachers and professors. In these cases, persistence has a positive effect. In healthy relationships, there's always a certain persistence so that all parties involved are benefitted.

Depending on how the situation goes, persisting can be negative for a person. Manipulators are experts in the act of insisting and wrapping the other person up, getting them to do what they want. In these cases, the person being the object of persistence doesn't get the acknowledgement or consideration they deserve.

One way to know if the person who's insisting has good or bad intentions when acting persistently is to ask the following questions:

- Are they requesting something that only benefits them?
- Is there a threat within the persistence they manifest?
- Are they sucking up to me in a malicious way inside their persistence trick?
- Are they using guilt in any way to get what they want?
- Do they express their persistence accompanied by the sentence "or else…"?

When the housework is assigned, it's common that one of the people has to insist that one of the members fulfills their tasks. This persistence is based on the benefit of the family's cohabiting. It can get to be manipulation in some cases, though the usual thing is that it's the necessary persistence to make the family organization work.

Generally, persistence is considered to be the key to professional success, and, therefore, economic success. It's a means to strengthen the character, the will and the self-esteem. It develops the sense of commitment, beliefs and the vision of the future. It also stimulates the patience needed to achieve a goal and not abandon it.

In the following examples you can appreciate people

who succeeded thanks to their persistence:

- Walt Disney: at the beginning he was rejected because he was considered to have no talent for cartoons. He said himself that the difference between winning or losing was not abandoning.
- The Wright brothers: they were incredibly criticized for wanting to build a machine that could fly. If it weren't for their persistence, they wouldn't have built their *Kitty Hawk* with which they made their famous first flight.
- Enrico Caruso: he was rejected by all the singing masters of his time being rendered talentless. He was self taught and he earned enormous fame.
- Bruce Lee: he was myopic, had a deviated spine and one leg was shorter than the other. This didn't stop him from becoming a Kung Fu master and creating his own martial art the *Jeet Kune Do*.

These examples clearly show the benefits you can get from being persistent. Always within certain boundaries you'll get positive results from having a goal as a community. The use of persistence involves more feeling than you could imagine. That's why the manipulator could find words that activate said feelings to achieve their purpose through persistence.

LOVE BOMBING AND SILENT TREATMENT

The "love bombing" is very used when trying to conquer a person. It's used not only in the case of chasing a love relationship, but when you expect to get to someone to achieve a close relationship as soon as possible. As we've seen in a previous section, it consists of exaggerated displays of affection to flatter the chosen person. When a manipulator Hope's to control a victim they will approach them, and without too many interactions they'll start their "love bombing" to show their interest.

Which is why, this unexpected bombing from someone you're just meeting, should be a call to attention since it's not usual that someone displays that much generosity and selflessness. If the victim lets themselves be wrapped up, they will be making it easier for the manipulator, who will combine it with other techniques which will lead to their subduing, losing their identity, their friendships, and most likely, their money and, as a consequence, their mental health.

This method is so effective that it's highly used by sexual predators when they're trying to approach teenagers. It's also used by religious leaders when they're trying to attract followers, especially lonely people. The "love bombing "makes them feel contained, wanted, noticed, definitely, they develop a sense of belonging to the faith that this leader is preaching.

The primary objective when applying this technique is

to reach the victim's heart earning their trust. Generally, the person applying it is a nice, charismatic person, with good manners who manages to easily enter an entertained conversation and makes the victim trust them and lower their guard.

In a vertiginous way they'll go from being a complete stranger to an almost essential person. The victim will open up and tell them about their lives, sharing valuable information that the manipulator will use in a later stage. They'll get to know their weak spots, preferences, personal and professional conflicts, affections and everything related to their world. They'll fill the victim with messages, calls, small gifts, beautiful phrases, poems which will overflow their heart with new emotions which are difficult to resist and that cloud the senses and numb reason. And, above all, their actions seem to overflow with sincerity.

Manipulators know how to detect people who have a greater need for affection or that live in loneliness or that have had a traumatic breakup. These people are easier to turn into victims because they have a previous need. When the person leads a life that's considered normal, it's more difficult to capture them and to manipulate them because their emotions are even and under control.

Those who use this technique, once they enter their victim's psyche, they start showing during conversations how similar they are and the great connection they feel going on between them. They can even say something like: "I am surprised I was lucky enough to meet you" or "we were made to be together, we were made for each other".

This system opens a door which leads straight to the heart, it doesn't give you time to think or analyze and those people who instinctively try to rationalize find themselves overwhelmed by a huge wave of love and flattery that's difficult to refuse. This "love bombing" is pretty much irresistible. It shows a lovely person, open, sensitive and highly generous who isn't afraid to show their feelings at all times and who inspires trust.

THE SILENT TREATMENT

This is another technique that has a lot to do with punishment. The manipulator acts in the following way: "If you don't do as I say I will take my love away". It can be used easily on people who have a great emotional dependency, or after having applied for some time the "love bombing". One you get the person to be emotionally dependent it's the ideal moment to use this technique. In work environments it's often used so that the person feels diminished, unnoticed, invaluable, and even nonexistent. This can affect, on a greater or lesser measure, depending on how strong their emotions are.

The one trying to control will request a favor or action from the victim and, if they refuse, the silent treatment will begin, completely ignoring them, as if they weren't there. The deeper the emotional relationship between them, the harder this will be on the victim. It is very likely that they'll change their minds and do what they've asked, even against their own will. It is very common that, if it worked the first time, the manipulator will use it again as many times as they need.

THREAT OF LOSING THE CONQUERED LOVE

If the person has been subjected to the love bombing, it is logical that they'll develop fear of losing that love or, if it's a rude put into play by a religious leader, they develop the fear of losing the position they've achieved within the group. To introduce the seed of fear and have it grown, the manipulator will use sentences such as: "I love you, but you need to understand that..." or "here's the position you've earned but the new member that came in...".

These sentences can be demolishing for some sensitive or emotionally fragile people's feelings. They will start going through their memory looking for what they could've done to make them angry and, surely, they'll find something to blame themselves about. It's possible they start apologizing and try to avoid at all costs any situation that keeps them in silence.

GENERATING GUILT

Guilt is a feeling which is generated within each person and sets a reference between what should be and what is, or what was done and what could've been done. It has deep roots since it is based on the education received as children, the taught values, how they were treated by the person who raised them and, generally, how they were treated by the whole family environment.

If the upbringing was strict, the feeling of guilt will be greater. According to the upbringing, a mental profile is made about how the behavior they need to adjust should be. Every time their behavior diverges from this mental pattern, it's very likely that they'll feel guilty. Each person will make their own elaboration of guilt according to their psychological characteristics and they'll project them on others in, probably, the same way they received them during their childhood.

The manipulator will use this to reach the deepest places in the victim's psyche, aside from making them remember all the rules they had to respect when they were little and which led them to be an adorable, lovable and, logically, politically correct little person.

Guilt triggers feelings of shame and repentance that are necessary to elaborate on and transcend in a healthy and positive way. Otherwise, it will be a starting point for the manipulator to try to intensify and blow out of proportion to manipulate the person.

Every human being has a determined level of guilt which is related to their level of self-demand: the greater the self-demanding, the greater the level of guilt they'll feel because this person expects to have a behavior that is closest to perfection. When they catch themselves in a behavior that is far from the perfection, they expect from themselves, they start feeling guilty. Guilt is also associated with feelings of anguish, fear, sadness, anxiety, uncertainty, etc.

A manipulator who is close enough to their victim and has talked to them will recognize these weaknesses and they'll take them into account to bring them up when it's time. The person will do what it takes to fix their mistake and be rid of that feeling. For example:

- Manipulating guilt to end the self-esteem of the person: the person who blames themselves for different things, generally, doesn't feel valuable.
- Continually reminding them of their mistakes: if the victim feels guilty for not being as perfect as they'd like to, highlighting their mistakes will increase their levels of guilt.
- Using rejection, the silent treatment or minimization: making the victim feel rejected for their mistakes will increase the guilt they feel. In the same way, if the silent treatment is applied on them, they'll feel guilty for making their victimizer mad. When it comes to minimization, they'll start feeling guilty for not being up to the circumstances.
- Using social isolation: making them notice that people walk away from them and that they do it because of their behavior and their ability to make mistakes.

Whatever the subject is, the person who knows how to manipulate will find the way to make you feel guilty or increase your levels of guilt. If critical thought was activated, the person could see the actual value of the comment made by the person who is trying to manipulate them. Noticing these subtleties is the first step to break free from a manipulator. It's important to notice what you're feeling to make an analysis and identify what's the inner process that triggered this feeling.

Another way to identify if someone is trying to manipulate you is paying attention to the conversations you have. If a person is constantly bringing up your mistakes, be it in a subtle or direct way, it's almost certain that this person is trying to manipulate you. One you've identified the manipulator, you must get away from them. If it's not possible to get away because they belong to a closer environment, you need to put into practice the fact of paying no mind to everything they say.

Another way of managing those thoughts which generate guilt is explaining the person making the comments that you've internally elaborated on your conflicts and what they're saying doesn't affect you anymore on an emotional level. Therefore, they shouldn't waste their energy because they won't be able to make you feel guilty.

INTIMIDATION

Intimidation is an action exerted on another person to bend their will through fear. It's carried out in a direct or indirect way with a subtle but very effective work. The most characteristic example is when a burglar tells a person to give them all their money while they point a gun at their victim. The goal is to subdue them in order to get what they're looking for.

The person who intimidates in a direct way shows themselves being angry or rabid, they yell out orders and act with a threatening attitude which is very difficult to contradict. They can apply it verbally or take it as far as being physically violent if the victim refuses and resists to cooperate.

Indirect or undercover intimidation, is seemingly kinder than the previous one, it's a slow and constant work that the manipulator does to avoid the people around the victim notice it until it's too late. They're also violent people, but they know how to control themselves in front of society, showing themselves as gentle and charismatic.

They're dangerous people because they know how to hide their nature very well and the victim starts to realize it once they're already in a relationship with them and it's difficult for them to get out of the place they were placed in by their victimizer. The victim manages to see the truth in the event that their psychological state allows them to. Sometimes, they're so damaged and their psychological element is unable to realize the hell they're living. People who indirectly intimidate know how to use many tricks, they're cold and calculated. They're methods are highly effective, achieving their goals in most cases.

Sometimes, intimidation has a positive effect. For example, it's been psychologically proven that if a person has the intention of shoplifting at a supermarket and they're suddenly stared at consistently by someone else, they'll feel so intimidated and acknowledge that they'll quit their actions. Their bad intentions make them think that everyone knows of their misdeed and in their minds, they start fantasizing how they'll turn into a victim if they carry on their purpose. That's the reason why in many shops they hang signs that say "caught on camera" to intimidate those who are conceiving to commit a crime.

In a boxing fight, the boxers stare at each other in an intimidating way and if one of the two gets intimidated, surely, they'll lose the psychological or mental fight. The simple fact of letting themselves be intimidated will make him have a smaller chance at winning than if they merely pay no mind to the intimidation. Generally, it is used so that the press has something to talk about and not to cause a psychological action on the other fighter. Definitely, it's a matter of Marketing.

There are bedtime stories which intimidate children into performing certain actions or else something bad will happen to them. A traditional children's song in Spanish speaking countries says: "Go to sleep baby, go to sleep now, or else you'll get eaten by the boogeyman". A sweet way to intimidate, if intimidation can get to be sweet.

Intimidation, when it's undercover, manages to convince the other victim that they're doing the right thing. On the other hand, direct intimidation through physical violence brings up feelings of hate or rebelliousness in the victim, and though its effects can be seen in plain sight, it is less traumatic than the intimidation that's carried out slowly and which deeply affects the victim's psyche. They will find it much harder to move on once their predator gets caught and they're free of them.

So that the control is maintained for an extended period of time, intimidation must be fed frequently and constantly. Aside from the sentences the manipulator uses, they make their body language match their intentions and it's capable of breaking one or many objects to give veracity to what they're saying. Violence, anger and conflict are their favorite tools since they have an important visual impact on the victim.

The victim tries to pacify the moment so it doesn't turn into an extreme situation. The reality is that they're afraid of them and they can't find a way to break free from this vicious cycle they find themselves in.

MANIPULATION OF THE FACTS

The manipulation of the facts is also a manipulation technique in itself, though it can be used in conjunction with others to achieve certain success. Manipulating a situation means that, using real facts, you give them a more convenient interpretation suppressing details, taking sentences out of context, increasing or decreasing the importance of certain attitudes. In this way, they distort what's happened without lying.

Language is so rich in hues that it allows a sentence to be said in different ways, or tell the same story in different versions. A skillful manipulator in the art of oratory or able to bend the facts to their will, even turning into the hero who saved the day.

Another example is the case of lawyers when they defend a criminal. They distort the facts to take responsibility away from the defendant. Generally, they do it so that their clients win the case or get a benefit out of the process.

Another way of applying the manipulation of facts is to make up excuses. This behavior is quite frequent when they want to avoid taking responsibility for what happened. Excuses are used in every order of life and are used at all ages. Every person at some point of their lives has made up an excuse and most times, they did it so they could avoid telling the truth.

Another way in which people manipulate what happened is blaming the victim because they're the ones who trigger the events. It's common to find this variation when a beating man tells his partner that it was her fault that he got angry and he didn't have any other choice than to beat her. It's generally more effective with victims that have been isolated from their surroundings and can't find someone to learn on. Also, it's very likely that they love their manipulator and justify them.

Another variation of facts' manipulation is withholding information or telling the facts in a strategic way. Knowing how the listener responds to a certain information, the manipulator will manage to handle the truth in a way that it turns out to be sensitive to the receiver. They'll also hide the details that aren't convenient for them to reveal. This variation of strategic narrative manipulation is very used by politicians. Their speeches are full of facts told in this way and details are being suppressed deliberately.

Finally, another way of manipulating the facts is to exaggerate certain parts of the story, making it sensationalist or taking importance away from it to the point of minimizing it. This technique is used by publicity, marketing agencies, public relations and in some media outlets. It's frequent to see the media accentuate some features in the information they're providing while hiding others. You can appreciate this, mainly, on the headlines they use with the intention of flashing the information they'll develop in their article.

Internationally, this technique has been used to discredit nations, introducing beliefs, changing behaviors. It was used during the cold war, also known as, psychological war. In every case, it will never be an objective story, they won't lie but they'll be telling a halfway truth from a subjective perspective.

HOW TO KNOW IF YOU'RE BEING MANIPULATED?

Generally, the person applying the manipulation is often a lovely, charismatic person and it's hard to recognize that their actions have bad intentions because they seem to be sincere and honest. Their work is subtle, elaborate, very well planned and their actions aren't noticed until some time has passed and their actions are analyzed.

Oftentimes, when filling emotional voids, the rational aspects of the manipulated person close off and they don't see what is really happening. The great skill the manipulator shows turns the victim into a puppet handled at their will. For these reasons, it's important to be attentive and learn how to see the signals which distinguish a manipulator. It's not necessary to know manipulation techniques to know if someone from your surroundings or a stranger is trying to manipulate you.

If you're in a relationship it's necessary to analyze the following points, in which you'll look at yourself, to know if the other person is manipulating you:

- When you go from the joy of having finally found love, but in a short amount of time this turns into fear of losing them. Your feelings of joy and happiness are suddenly feelings of sadness, anguish and desperation.
- Your emotions don't have a middle ground, you go from a feeling of completeness to a filling of void without mediating conflicting situations.
- You stay in the relationship even though most of the time you don't feel happy with it. Being happy went from being something constant to being something sporadic.
- You feel responsible for every situation that happens, even when you have nothing to do with it.
- You start feeling guilty for the other person's unhappiness.
- You're aware that the relationship has turned complex and you don't know how you got to that point.
- You're obsessed by the relationship to the point where you talk about it with everybody all the time, whether

it's a friend, an acquaintance or a stranger who was just passing by.

- You're continuously defensive, guard up high, in a general belligerent state, which generates you a lot of anxiety.
- You feel jealousy, insecurity, any person that approaches your partner you see as a potential enemy.
- You have the need to be vigilant about where they spend their day, the messages in their phone, their social media, their search history, their email, etc.
- You start feeling like you don't make your partner happy, you might also feel like you don't deserve them, uncertainty surrounds your life and anxiety is constantly present.
- You try not to talk to your partner about what's bothering you, you put on a happy face so that your real feelings are covered.
- The fear of being apart is greater every time.
- You sabotage the relationship almost unconsciously and then you start wondering why you did it.
- You go through outbursts of anger, you think you can control it but you realize you fall into them over and over again.
- You're able to do things that go against your values so that your partner is happy and the relationship continues.

This doesn't mean that all the signs need to be present. If some of them are, it's enough reason to start thinking you're being manipulated. It's also recommended that you do a professional consultation so that you can heal and close all of these patterns, so they won't come up in your next relationship.

The first feeling they'll develop on you will be confusion. The manipulator will make you doubt yourself: you'll believe your intuition is off, you won't know if you're making the right choices, the messages you get from your partner, whether they're verbal or nonverbal, will be confusing.

Then you'll start making an effort to comprehend what you're doing wrong, analyzing what you're about to say because you don't want your partner to react badly. You'll start feeling alone, like you're isolated from the world. The manipulator will try to get you away from your friends in order to control you. This will lead you to behave in a submissive, obedient and irrational way. At times, your friends, who are starting to notice what's going on, will try to warn you but you won't listen because you think they're wrong. If the person who's with you wants to manipulate you, they'll do everything they can to plant insecurity in your brain and your actions. Your self-esteem will hang from a thread.

Differentiating the kind of person that those who you deal with often, and that which you chose as a partner is, will allow you to not fall into manipulation. This way, you'll manage to move around healthy relationships and even heal those who are sick.

WHO MANIPULATE US?

Manipulation can be exerted in the different orders of life. In this section you can see different types of manipulators.

Salesmen and their use of the art of manipulation

Salesmen introduce their merchandise in a way that's attractive for customers. Whether they sell clothing, travels, cars, books, shows, they'll try to get the customer to buy what they're selling. When the salesman guides their customer, they're not looking for their own benefit but to help the customer get a product that's convenient for them. Though, they're making a sale, they do so without influencing but by giving their best advice. When the salesman persuades their customer to buy the most expensive product, in that case, they are using manipulation.

There are 4 types of salesmen according to *The manipulation of men through language* by Alfonso López Quintás: the salesmen of power, the salesmen of money, the salesmen of prestige and the salesmen of ideas and attitudes.

The salesmen of power are those who promise benefits in exchange for getting their votes. These are politicians that, no matter the ideology, culture or country, act by exerting the power of persuasion. To them, people are simply voters.

The salesmen of money seduce people to buy regardless of whether they actually need the product or not. They're only interested in the economic benefit and to them, everyone's a customer.

The salesmen of prestige look for public acknowledgement from everyone else and they want them to become admirers of their shows or texts.

The salesmen of ideas and attitudes have the ability to prove that their values and philosophies are worthy of being taken into account and adopted as their own. They seduce with their ideas and lead people to modify their behaviors. Their leaders by nature who, at times could be positive, but that most times, turn out to be negative without their followers noticing it.

For example, a person that's only interested in dressing well will surely not care about reading a good book. Therefore, as much as you introduce it in an attractive way, it's very possible they won't buy it. However, if you offer them an item from an Oscar De La Renta collection, they might even indent themselves so they can buy it. There's an audience for everything, though great salesmen have the ability to create the necessity of buying the object they are selling. Trying to change the mindset and tastes individually is difficult. Which is why those who know marketing work to create a consumption culture. There was a time in which drinking and smoking was advertised as a way to get social relationships. That way, it's also been established that a person is successful when they have a well-paid job, a family, a home, one or two cars and go out on vacation every year. If something's not fulfilled it can even be considered that the person got stuck in life.

Another example is the publicity that glorifies youth, which makes many people do whatever it takes to look young even if they have no possible way to hide their age. That same culture condemns the elderly as the mere fact of growing old is shameful.

Manipulation and machiavellian ideologies

People who seek to manipulate lifestyle ideologies don't seek a foundation for what they want to achieve but they rely on their cleverness to shape and defeat popular opinion. They manage to turn concepts around, mark reality planes, turn ideas around avoiding getting caught aside from achieving their goals. You can find ideological manipulation in the study plans, media outlets, political speeches, etc.
We mustn't forget the great emotional burden that ideologies which facilitate other's acceptance end up having. They become so strong that they're able to divide nations, towns and even families. However, the pandemic in recent times has shown that it knows no boundaries, frontiers, ideologies or social classes and the separations that human beings achieve so meticulously can be knocked down in a single stroke and that the only important thing is the true essence of humanity.

Manipulation on the hands of businessmen

Businessmen, as of today, have an important role in social development. It's a position that demands talent, an entrepreneurial spirit and determination to face the risks. It's a position of power which requires us to provide answers for the market's demands and to the great competition they face.

For most of the businessmen, their employees are the "human resource" which will allow them to achieve their goals. The employee is a simple gear in their machinery system and they're only interested in keeping them "oiled up" so that they work correctly.

How scientists manipulate

Scientists have their own way of manipulating events, behaviors, beliefs by subjecting them to a rigorous scientific vision. It's common to hear that reality can only be checked through science and that all that can't be explained in that way —like the existence of a God or the soul's immortality—, belongs to the irrational aspects of the human being. It's necessary that science takes on a humbler position and recognizes their limitations.

Manipulation in education

In tyranny times, it's common that they try to maintain the population in a low educational level. This happens, because when the educational processes aren't the most adequate, critical judgement stays at a low level and the population becomes easy to manipulate.

This way, in governments who claim to be democratic and hope to defeat without having to convince, study plans are made in a way that they don't motivate students to develop the ability to think, discern, their intellectual curiosity and all things that makes a human being able to analyze their reality.

A person who has developed their critical judgement won't be easily stepped over, and is not easy prey for a manipulator.

CONCLUSION

As you can appreciate, being the victim of manipulation has serious consequences, that's why it's important to always bear in mind that:

- A manipulator uses all their skills to achieve their goals, impoverishing the victim's life and making them vulnerable.
- Seduction can be so enveloping that it impedes rational thought.
- The seduced person often loses their identity, dignity and, sometimes, their personal values.
- The manipulator reduces the person to their minimal expression so they can have them under their control.
- The manipulator is an artist of language, which is why their words seem to be true, honest and generous, but you must keep in mind that they have the ability to exert demagogy and convince.

The victim debates between actual reality and the fiction their manipulator created for them. They find themselves alone, with no support from their family, doubting themselves and anguished, not being truly aware of what is going on. The victim, with their disrupted values, gives themselves to instinctive processes believing that is the only way to feel complete. They forget that plenitude is achieved through the values which, the higher they are, will show a richness in hues that separates the human being apart from the fallacies that a manipulator might be trying to plant.

In this way, by disrupting values and avoiding population to achieve a balanced education you return to primitive stages in which immediate satisfaction becomes valid. If, also, the future projection for the youth is scarce or nonexistent, you reach a breaking point in which delinquency increases, fanaticism grows and society, in general, falls into decay.

Human beings who have fallen victim to manipulators, will surely need the help of a mental health professional who understands that they must collaborate with the psychological liberation of these victims. They'll have to show them the path that manipulation often takes and the damages it causes on the mind as it moves forward. The victim, on the other hand, will have to learn the process that leads to understanding and discerning of what happened. It's necessary that the victim understands the way in which their reality has been distorted and what were the points they touched in order to achieve it.

Being aware of every person's weak spot, as well as their strengths will give them a vision of themselves and will also show them in which way a manipulator can enter their mind. Learning the different models of reality in which a manipulator can submerge their victim can give a better perspective to achieve the necessary preparation to not fall into the tricks of these kinds of individuals. At last, getting back the ideals and working to achieve a purpose of life will, finally, set the victim on track.

If you're in control of your mind, you know how you think and how you react, it's very difficult for someone to manipulate you. Besides, you'll be able to detect these types of individuals and warn the unsuspecting around you to stop them from being manipulated.

When there's real communication, when there's self-less principles that lead nations or human groups, the real flourishing of humanity is achieved. Knowing how much a thought can influence other people, it's time to take the choice to use it to achieve the common good and healthy and fruitful personal relationships.